Dancing on the Edge of the World

Jewish Stories of Faith, Inspiration, and Love

Edited and Collected by
Miriyam Glazer, Ph.D.

ROXBURY PARK

LOWELL HOUSE

LOS ANGELES

NTC/Contemporary Publishing Group

For my Parents,

Ida and Harry Glazer

"First Time Today"

Published by Lowell House
A division of NTC/Contemporary Publishing Group, Inc.
4255 West Touhy Avenue, Lincolnwood (Chicago), Illinois 60712-1975 U.S.A.

Lowell House books can be purchased at special discounts when ordered in bulk for premiums and special sales. Contact Department CS at the following address:
NTC/Contemporary Publishing Group
4255 West Touhy Avenue
Lincolnwood, IL 60712-1975
1-800-323-4900

ISBN: 0-7373-0388-3
Library of Congress Catalog Card Number: 99-76871

Roxbury Park is a division of NTC/Contemporary Publishing Group, Inc.

Managing Director and Publisher: Jack Artenstein
Editor in Chief, Roxbury Park Books: Michael Artenstein
Director of Publishing Services: Rena Copperman
Director of Art Production: Bret Perry
Editorial Assistant: Nicole Monastirsky
Interior Design: Stacie Chaiken

Printed and bound in the United States of America
99 00 01 02 DHD 10 9 8 7 6 5 4 3 2 1

PLEASANT WORDS ARE LIKE HONEYCOMB,
SWEET TO THE SOUL, HEALTH TO THE BONES.

—*PROVERBS 16:24*

Dancing on the Edge of the World is the second anthology in Roxbury Park's *New Visions* series, bringing to readers cutting-edge writings in psychology, spirituality, science, literature, and the arts. *New Visions* series editor: Mark Robert Waldman

also by Miriyam Glazer

Burning Air and a Clear Mind

*Dreaming the Actual: Contemporary Fiction
and Poetry by Israeli Women Writers*

also by Mark Robert Waldman:

The Art of Staying Together

Love Games

*Dreamscaping: New and Creative Ways
to Work with Your Dreams*

Contents

Acknowledgements

The idea of creating *Dancing on the Edge of the World* was first proposed to me by Mark Waldman, for whose inspiration, continued editorial guidance, and ready responses to my own odd sense of humor I am very grateful.

I am particularly grateful to my daughter, Avigail Glazer-Schotz, for her stellar editorial insights which, when directed to something I wrote, were not, shall we say, always willingly received–even though they were nearly always accepted. Her research and editorial assistance have been invaluable, along with her own delightful humor.

And, finally, I want to express my deep gratitude to the many contributors to *Dancing on the Edge of the World* for so graciously sharing the stories and poems culled from their own spiritual journeys. In the end, it is the eloquence of their souls that has created the book, and I thank them.

Introduction

Holy stories are the light of the world.
—Yitzhak Buxbaum

A leaky pot, rim dented, white enamel worn—stand it on the shelf next to the bamboo steamers and the wok? throw it out? or donate it to a museum, for it is the very pot in which your aging mother cooked her borscht in postwar Poland and then New York, and "Believe me it tells the quintessential twentieth-century Jewish story"?

Sing "Hatikvah" in the school auditorium—when you're the only Jewish kid in the school?

Find yourself in a Tel Aviv cab with Jane Fonda, responding to *her* story by sharing how memories of Auschwitz seeped into the underground streams of *your* life?

It's Hanukkah, and you're making latkes—recalling the story of your great-grandmother who, in an east European *shtetl* on Hanukkah eve a hundred years ago, opened the door to face a Cossack, there to take her son into the Czar's army.

Give hundreds of eloquent sermons on the meaning of Shabbat to your congregants, only to discover that you never really grasped the true meaning of the day until you began walking to shul with your sweet autistic son. . . .

Like an ecstatic artist, an adoring Jewish mother, God gazed out at the living creatures of the newly created Earth and declared, "Be fruitful and multiply!" By creating us in the Divine Image and giving us Torah, perhaps God meant to add, "and, like me, tell stories."

For Torah, the living tree of the Jewish people, overflows with stories. Beginning with its wondrous account, rippling with joy and generosity, of the Creation of the world, Torah relates riveting family dramas; tales of courage, prophetic vision, betrayal, and loyalty; the whole saga of the Hebrew people learning to cast off an internalized slavery and embrace the covenant at Sinai. Triumph, loss, redemption, wails of protest, hosannas to the Highest, the interpretation of dreams. No wonder that ours is a storytelling tradition: to unravel even the subtle minutiae of Torah law, the sages of ancient Israel told stories.

We are passionate about stories. They are traces within us of holiness, of the Divine Image in which we were formed. Through the ages, we have told stories to fathom the intensities our own collective history, to express our faith and our fears, to grasp the complexities of our religious tradition, to cast light on the mysteries of life. Stories have helped us to endure hard times. They have enabled us to share with one another what wisdom we have managed to accrue through life's journey—and the delights and dangers of that journey itself.

As the collection took shape, I rediscovered how much we have to share with one another, and how strong the longing to share it. From Israel and the States, stories poured in from rabbis, poets, scholars, students, storytellers, mystics, community leaders, journalists, actors: the sheer *plenitude* of it, the glorious *power* of it. Once again I found myself feeling the awe that the prayer so wonderfully expresses: *kakha lo b'olamo / so it is in God's universe!* Seeking to organize it all, I came to see that whether their source was deeply observant or more secular, the poems and stories and traditional commentaries spoke to one another across worlds, sensibilities, centuries. An ancient tale criticizes the revered spiritual leader Shimon bar Yochai for his fanaticism, while a prominent contemporary rabbi celebrates the value of uncertainty in religious faith ("Perhaps"), and a poet gazes with awe at the passionate Judaism of converts ("The Converts"). "The broken tablets were also carried in the ark," another poem reminds us, suggesting that the mistakes we have made, the losses we have suffered, our own shattered hopes, are not discarded as we journey to the "promised land." As both "Pay Attention" and "Spiritual Secrets" so beautifully reveal in their very different ways, the very brokenness of the tablets is precisely what can lead to a vital spiritual transformation. In "Playing with Three Strings," a concert by violinist Yitzhak Perlman teaches us how to transcend loss, how to play out, with all our heart, soul, and might, "the song left for us to sing."

The youth shall see visions, says the Bible. The little girl in "Raindrops" discovers God as she gazes out the rain-swept window in the family kitchen, and imagines that "somewhere in the world" another little girl is gazing out of *her* window imagining another little girl gazing out of *hers*. . . . The young Russian orphan in "A Plane Truth" puzzles his teachers by obsessively flying paper planes across the room, until they discover what the planes mean to him. In "Torquemada," another young boy is tortured by dreams that he has become Nebuchadnezzar sacking Jerusalem, Herod, Haman, Pharaoh, the Grand Inquisitor Torquemada, and only when he is comforted by his father do we realize the terrifying implications of those dreams. Even children, who cannot name the demons adults know, can sense their presence, as "Alligators Under the Bed" tells us.

Yet even in the grimmest darkness, a miraculous light can somehow shine. "In Days Gone By and in Our Own Time" takes us into a concentration camp in December 1943, watching a prisoner risking his life to kindle a Hanukkah candle. In "Hovering Above the Pit," a Jew with a revered rabbinical lineage is forced by the Nazis either to jump over a vast open pit or be shot. He survives.

Between the pages of these contemporary stories, the prophets and sages of ancient Israel and the Hasidic masters of eastern Europe intervene, commenting, cajoling, illuminating. On the night of his *yahrzeit*, the spirit of the Hasidic master Rabbi Nachman of Bratslav hovers over the writer, in the tale "Rabbi Nachman and I." Witnessing the birth of his daughter, a young professor weaves profound yet troubling lines from the Talmud into his new fatherhood as, filled with love, he welcomes her to the wisdom of Judaism. . . .

The biblical prophet Micah urges us to "seek justice"; Rabbi Eliezer ben Azariah warns us that wisdom must be expressed in deeds. Across the centuries, a progressive rabbi relates how a political protest leads him and a group of Evangelical Christian ministers to envision a new interdenominational "God's House" together.

Laugh? Cry? "My eyes fill with tears every time I read that. It's so *beautiful*," my twenty-two-year-old daughter says, as she looks up from her third reading of the tender story, "God's Perfection." Every time I read "Song," I find myself laughing at the wild, inveterately Jewish humor, well aware at the same time of the heartbreak woven into the story's lines.

"God loves things which are complex and beautiful / which move and change and turn," declares the opening poem of the book.

> *God loves cycles*
> *which fit together in ingenious ways, epic poems, the rain,*
> *the reading of Torah, the passing of seasons,*
> *photosynthesis, death. God loves things which explode.*
> *Today, God sent the angels to observe a supernova,*
> *and we were not far behind. Wonder of wonders!*
> *Our microscopes and telescopes are temples.*
> *This is the world God chose to use and mend,*
> *the world which we discover with our senses. . . .*

The stories and poems in this book help us to discover that world with our *Jewish* senses, to tell the tale of both the explosions and the tender mercies we have witnessed. For *Wonder of Wonders!* having been dancing on the edge of the world for thousands of years, can we Jews tell a story!

JILL HAMMER

Yehi Meorot Barakia: "Let There Be Lights in the Expanse"

Who needs myth? The star struggling
out of the lips of a nebula is enough,
the pink coral, the frog with translucent feet,
the fish making love on a leaf above the Amazon,
the migrating salmon, the bee dancing,
geodes, constellations, Venice!

Jerusalem. The clouds pretending to be sheep
and the sheep pretending to be clouds.
The camera of the eye. The breaking down of sugar.
The placental embrace of mother and child.
The hummingbird and the trumpet-flower.
The illness which causes one to sneeze
and the one which is an assassin, and the cure.
The blue topaz and the neurosis. The tadpole
growing legs, and the starfish when it loses one,
the spiraling horns of the ibex, and coal burning.

Let us declare the awesome power of the sun
and the earth which tilts around it.
Let us bless the source of tides, the moon
which taught us to number our days.
God loves things which are complex and beautiful,

Jill Hammer

which move and change and turn. God loves cycles
which fit together in ingenious ways, epic poems, the rain,
the reading of Torah, the passing of seasons,
photosynthesis, death. God loves things which explode.

Today, God sent the angels to observe a supernova,
and we were not far behind. Wonder of wonders!
Our microscopes and telescopes are temples.
This is the world God chose to use and mend,
the world which we discover with our senses.
This is the tail of the comet, the dust, the bright color
which points us in the invisible direction.
This is the bread of God; we eat it with our eyes.

Jill Hammer is a rabbinical student at the Jewish Theological Seminary, and the editor of the journal of contemporary midrash, Living Text.

The Legacy

On a cold December day in 1889, during the festival of Hanukkah, in a small *shtetl* in Lithuania, Rachel Reva Hassel wrapped her shawl around her shoulders. She carried a large bag filled with potatoes and onions home from the market. Her small frame looked even smaller under the heavy load. A faint smile crept on her lips as she thought about the potato latkes she would make later in the day. Hanukkah was one of her favorite times of year. Suddenly the clippity clippity clippity of a fleet-footed horse could be heard from a distance, a different hoofbeat than that of the slow workhorses from her village. Swifter, lighter, the sound grew louder and closer. Soon Rachel Reva spotted the Cossack soldier on horseback, the shiny buttons on his uniform glistening in the wintry sun. Her eyes filled with terror as he leaned over his horse in full stride and scooped up a small boy wearing a long black coat and a flat cap. A *yidele* just walking home from *cheder.* The little boy flailed his arms and legs, struggling and screaming, as his desperate mother ran after the horse pleading, "Stop! Stop!"

Rachel Reva put down her heavy load and ran to comfort the hysterical mother. They both knew the boy would be taken to a non-Jewish family until he was old enough to serve in the Czar's army. Rachel Reva had witnessed the kidnapping of the little Jewish boys many times. They were rarely ever seen again.

On her way home, she tried to convince herself that her own sons were safe, that they were street-smart, good runners. "Our family has always been blessed with *mazel*," she murmured to herself. "These things happen only to others." Still, the horse had come so close to her that she could feel the dust he kicked up in her face, and the screams and tears had pierced her heart.

She arrived home just in time to peel and grate potatoes for latkes. In the evening they lit the *shammas* and the first candle of the menorah in the window, and sang the blessings. The children sat down on the floor to play dreidel. In the soft light she gazed at her husband, and thought to herself that what the neighbors said was true: with his long white beard, he looked more like a rabbi than like the tailor he was. But as she was gazing, she heard the dreaded hoofbeats she had heard too many times before. They were coming closer and closer. Her family fell silent. Heavy boots crunched the snow. Rachel Reva stood up. Her breath stopped. A loud, insistent knock on her neighbor's door.

A heart-piercing scream, shuffling feet, and the trotting of horses into the distance.

The Cossack had grabbed young Yankele Bernstein. Rachel Reva's children searched their parents' eyes for comfort. "The Cossacks won't come back," she told them. "The army is full now and God has blessed this family with more *mazel* than most." But it was hard even for her to believe those words.

That night she lay awake in bed. The sounds of the latest scream etched in her memory did not disappear so quickly. She tossed and turned until daybreak. Then she arose, went to the market, and bought a piece of heavy brown fabric. All afternoon she sewed curtains for the windows. Knowing that her family had to light the Hanukkah candles, she convinced herself that at least the curtains would keep the candlelight in the house, hidden from the street.

That night, Rachel Reva lit the menorah with her family. The light stayed inside the house and the family felt safe. The children sat down to a quick game of dreidel before dinner while she went into the kitchen to check on the latkes. Clippity clippity clippity . . . the hoofbeats came closer. Clippity clippity clippity . . . the hoofbeats stopped. The crunch of boots on snow. And then the terrible knock on the Hassel family door.

Rachel Reva did not cower or bow her head. She breathed in the light from those candles and it made her feel as though she stood six feet tall. She opened the door. The Cossack stood there before her. Rachel Reva looked right into his eyes.

"We've been expecting you," she said. "So don't just stand there, dinner is ready. The food will get cold."

The Cossack felt the hunger rise in his belly. He stepped inside wordlessly, took off his coat, lay his bayonet next to the door, and sat down to eat at Rachel Reva's table.

Rachel Reva stacked a plateful of latkes in front of him. He stared at the glowing faces of the family one by one. White beard, side locks, little girl braids, little boy rosy cheeks.

"Eat, *kinder*, eat!" insisted Rachel Reva.

The Cossack ate and sipped tea and ate and sipped more tea. When his plate was empty, Rachel Reva piled on more latkes and demanded that he eat again. Not until he couldn't lift his fork for another bite did she stop.

When he finally rose from the table, he grinned broadly, patted his full belly, put his coat back on, and picked up his bayonet. The bayonet was all he took with him when he left.

The two Hassel sons grew up to be tailors like their papa and the two daughters emigrated to America. The youngest, Ida, became my grandmother. She never forgot that Hanukkah in the *shtetl* and the courage of her mother, Rachel Reva. Ida passed on the story— and Rachel Reva's recipe for latkes—to her daughter, who was my mother, who passed them both on to me.

Now I have two daughters of my own. They are still young. But someday, when they are ready, I will pass on the legacy of Rachel Reva, who taught us that a mother's passion to save her children can ignite the kindness, wisdom, and fierce courage to know that even within an enemy soldier may lurk the hunger of a boy.

....

USA Today *wrote that "Karen Golden's mesmerizing stories marry age-old values with rollicking saxophone and amazing sound effects. You'll find the tunes, the tastes and the traditions of Jewish people from Eastern Europe to the Santa Monica Pier." Audiences from coast to coast have applauded her work as a performer, writer, teacher, and recording artist. Her biggest stories, daughters Hyla and Soli, are in process.*

GOD'S PERFECTION

In Brooklyn, New York, there is a school, *Chush*, for learning-disabled Jewish children. One evening, at a fund-raising dinner for the school, the father of one of the *Chush* children arose, extolled the school and its dedicated staff, and then cried out: "We are taught that God is perfect and all that God does is done with perfection. But what about my son, Shaya? He cannot understand things as other children do. He cannot remember facts and figures as other children do. Where is the Divine Perfection in Shaya?"

Shocked by the question, pained by the father's anguish, the audience sat in silence as he went on.

"Perhaps," he continued, "I have found the answer to my own question."

And he told a story:

One Sunday afternoon, Shaya and his father came to the yeshiva where Shaya studies in the morning. The yeshiva boys were playing baseball.

"I would like to be in the game," Shaya whispered to his father. His father was worried—he knew Shaya was not athletic at all, that he didn't even know how to hold a bat properly, let alone hit a ball with it—and that most of the boys understandably wouldn't want his son on their team.

Nevertheless, he approached one of the boys in the field and asked if Shaya might join them.

The boy shrugged. "We're losing by six runs, and we're already in the eighth inning. So I guess it's okay if he joins our team and goes up to bat for us in the ninth!"

Shaya and his father were both ecstatic.

But by the bottom of the eighth, Shaya's team had managed to hit three runs and by the bottom of the ninth they scored again. When Shaya's turn at bat came up, they had two outs and the bases were loaded. Would they really let Shaya go to bat now?

They did.

The first pitch came in. Shaya swung clumsily and missed.

One of the teammates came up to Shaya and helped him hold the bat.

The pitcher took a few steps forward. He threw the ball softly — and the two batters together hit a slow grounder.

The pitcher caught the ball and could have easily ended the whole game by throwing it to the first baseman.

Instead, he threw it on a high arc to right field, way beyond the first baseman's reach.

"Shaya, run to first! Run to first!" all the boys yelled.

Never in his life had Shaya ever had to "run to first."

Wide-eyed, startled, he scampered down the baseline. By the time he reached first, the right fielder had the ball. He could have easily thrown it to the second baseman who in turn would tag Shaya out, but instead he threw it far over the third baseman's head.

Everyone started yelling again, "Shaya, run to second! Run to second!"

Shaya ran to second base as the runners ahead of him deliriously circled the bases toward home. When he got to second base, the other team's shortstop ran up to him, turned him toward third base, and shouted, "Shaya, Shaya, run to third!"

And then as he rounded third, all the boys from both teams ran behind him screaming, "Shaya, run home! Shaya, run home!"

And Shaya ran home. No sooner had he stepped on home plate than all the boys from both of the teams raised him high in the air on their shoulders. He had just hit a "grand slam" and won the game for his team.

"That day," said the father, who by now had tears rolling down his face, "I learned about God's perfection. For when God brings a child like Shaya into the world, the perfection God seeks is in how other people treat him."

Paysach J. Krohn

Paysach J. Krohn is a rabbi and fifth-generation mohel in Brooklyn, New York. He is the author of Echoes of the Maggid: Heartwarming Stories and Parables of Wisdom and Inspiration *(Mesorah Publications, 1999), among other collections of inspirational stories.*

A Soldier's Sabbath

At our house, the seventh day
isn't quite what it is
in the book of Genesis.
The division between sacred and profane
is measured
differently:

how many days left . . . how many days before . . .
how many days till . . .

grasping a pass in his hand,
setting his gun down at the front door,
switching his fatigues for a tee shirt,
resting his head on his father's shoulder
and mine,
my son Iyar comes home
from the army.
Only then are the heavens and earth
and all that is within them finished
and I bless the Sabbath candles,
and we rest.

Come my beloved, groom of the Sabbath
Crowned by his homecoming, any day
is sacred—
Fribath—
Tuesbath—

Nava Semel

Thursbath—
A *whole week* home, and we replay
the saga of creation from
chaos and the void
to Adam wrought in the Divine Image.
There was darkness on the face of the deep.
Now there is light.

Watch over him for me, King of the universe.
Blessed are You who gives us purpose in life.
Praised are You
who hallows the Sabbath of soldiers.

Translated from the Hebrew by Miriyam Glazer

Israeli Nava Semel has written fiction, plays, scripts, and librettos,
most recently Nightgames (Am Oved, 1994), *about forty-something*
Israelis, and Bride on Paper (Am Oved, 1995), *which takes place in*
Palestine during the 1930s. She won the National Jewish Book
Award for Becoming Gershona (1990) *and the Israeli Prime*
Minister Award for Literature (1996).

Alligators Under
the Bed

I learned most of my theology not from my teachers but from my children. When my daughter Nessa was three years old, we had a routine. Each night I would tuck her into bed, sing our bedtime prayers, kiss her good night, and attempt to sneak out of the room. When I was halfway down the hall, she began to scream:

"Abba! There's an alligator under my bed! There's a monster in the closet! There's a giant spider on the ceiling! Abba!"

An avid reader of the Torah of Parenting, *Parents Magazine,* I know what to do: I walk back to the child's room and turn on every light. I look under the bed.

"No alligator, Nessa." I check the closet. "No monsters, Nessa." I survey the ceiling. "No spiders, Nessa. Now go to bed. Tomorrow is coming and you've got to get to sleep. Everything is safe. Good night."

"OK, Abba," she agrees. "But leave a light on."

Nessa and I did this dance for an entire year until one night I stopped myself as I walked down the hall. I asked myself who was right. Whose description of the world was empirically, factually, correct? The child afraid of alligators under the bed? Or the father who reassures her that everything is safe and tomorrow is surely coming?

The truth is that it is the child. She doesn't know the names of the alligators under the bed. She doesn't know about cancer, about AIDS, about drive-by shootings and lunatics who steal children. We grown-ups, we know their names, and yet we still insist to our children that the world is safe enough to trust for this one night.

All loving parents do this. Even the most hard-boiled atheists say to their kids, "Tomorrow is coming, you're safe tonight, go to sleep."

That faith is the beginning of spirituality, of our experience of God's presence. Adolescents can proclaim their disbelief. It's easy for them—they don't put children to bed each night. They're isolated—there is no one whose life and hope depends upon them. But those of us who live with others, who live for others, we know better. Having children, raising children, loving another with all our soul is an exercise in spirituality.

Spirituality is not something added onto life. It is underneath life, just beneath the surface of consciousness. It represents the answers to the ultimate questions of our lives—questions we may never have consciously asked, but whose answers ring through our daily actions. Why do we get out of bed in the morning? Where do we find the hope, strength, inspiration to go on each day? How do we cope with all that's terrifying in life?

Judaism is a way, a language, for asking these questions consciously. It is a way of sharing the answers of the generations that have come before us. And it is a discipline for facing our fears, listening to the questions, and searching out the answers.

....

Ed Feinstein serves as a rabbi of Valley Beth Shalom in Encino, California, and as a lecturer in the Ziegler School of Rabbinic Studies at the University of Judaism in Los Angeles. His Torah commentaries appear in the Los Angeles Jewish Journal. *Well known for his storytelling, Rabbi Feinstein is reputed to bake the best challach west of the Rio Grande, according to wife Rabbi Nina Feinstein and children Yonah (14), Nessa (11), and Raphael (8).*

WAR AND PEACE

After our two-year stint as graduate students in the States and several weeks of gallivanting through Europe, my husband and I arrived at the port of Piraeus—only to discover that our ship home to Israel was nowhere to be found. Attributing it to the vagaries of Greek bureaucracies, off we went to the Tourist Police.

The thickly mustached policeman on duty grinned.

"Boom Boom Israel! Boom Boom! Why you want go Israel?"

Then he pulled out his Greek newspaper, with its blaring headlines. "E—GIP—TUS," we made out. Tanks. Maps showing arrows drawn across the Suez Canal.

My husband and I stared at one another in disbelief. "There's a war!"

"I have to join my unit," he said.

By three the next morning we were landing in an unmarked plane in the blacked-out airport near a darkened Tel Aviv. Army officers were waiting in Arrivals; my husband signed in, and all he was permitted to tell me was that they were sending him "Somewhere in Israel." Suddenly alone, dazed by this ragged transformation from gaily vacationing American grad student to worried Israeli soldier's wife, I made my way in the middle of the night to Jerusalem, wondering where I'd stay.

The war dragged on for weeks, a brutal, demoralizing, nightmare for the country. The shock of it; the exposed vulnerability; the anguish and rage over the military disorder. Stories of slaughter, of soldiers dying of thirst in the Sinai. The hospitals were crowded with desperately wounded soldiers, friends, friends of friends. The Syrian army, notorious for its brutality, had taken a colleague's son prisoner. The twin sons of our distant cousins were both killed.

"You want to be men, or no? You want to be men or no?" a maddened young man cried out obsessively on downtown Ben Yehuda Street.

The Yom Kippur War marked the end of an era: the years of heady confidence that the country had bathed in since the victory of 1967 came to a bitter, chaotic halt. Those of us who had been exhilaratingly young before the war abruptly aged.

But it wasn't until four years later, when I gave birth to my daughter in Hadassah Hospital in Jerusalem, that I discovered how deep the scars of the Yom Kippur War could go.

I went into labor Seder night, 1977. The labor, though, went on for so many hours that the midwife insisted on giving me an infusion, and the infusion in turn half knocked me out. "PUSH!" she commanded and, jolted out of my daze, I pushed with every ounce of strength my body could muster, passed out, awoke to "PUSH!" and pushed and pushed and pushed again. By the time my daughter uttered her first victorious cry of life I was utterly spent.

Then she was gone: before I had a chance to hold her, she was whisked away from me and I was wheeled off to the crowded maternity ward.

I fell into a drugged stupor and awoke the next morning just as the nurses rolled in the carts of babies ready for their breakfast.

They called out the women's names one by one.

"Ben Oren?" *Yah!* "Mizrachi?" *"Khan/Here!"*

"Hevroni? Bar Cohen? Schulman?"

My anxiety rose. Why weren't they calling my name? What had happened to my baby?

"Where's *my* baby?" I cried out in my still-awkward Hebrew, by now nearly hysterical. "Where's *my* baby?"

Hadassah Hospital's Finest shrugged, asked my name, checked her list, and shrugged again, "I dund know."

"WHO KNOWS?"

She mumbled something and disappeared while, ribs aching and genitals burning from stitches, I struggled to crawl off the bed.

"Your daughter," she said when she returned, "is *bah pah gee yah.*"

A ferocity awoke in me I had never known I possessed. "In *pah gee yah?*" I knew the word from the newspaper accounts of the war: *wounded. My daughter was wounded!*

Desperate to rescue her, I ran pain-by-pain out of the maternity ward, hobbling down a long corridor until I came to a big room. I pulled open the glass doors. Before me were rows upon rows of newborns in plastic cradles, most of them sound asleep. Misshapen heads, puffy faces, IVs. My heart pounded.

"Where's my baby?" I screamed in English to the nurse on duty. "Why is she in the Wounded Baby Ward? What happened to her? What's wrong?"

The nurse gazed at me, strangely, kindly, and pointed out a sweetly sleeping tiny newborn girl with a shock of thick black newborn hair. Seeing her for the first time, I was flooded with love.

"Your daughter is fine," the nurse explained gently. "She's here because she's just a little small."

Her words bewildered me. *Just a little small?* I reached out to pick up my daughter and nestle her to my breast, and only then did it dawn on me: this wasn't the "Wounded Baby Ward." There *is* no such thing as a Wounded Baby Ward. "Wounded" in Hebrew was *p'goo'ah*; all that *pah'gee'yah* meant was "premature." My daughter had arrived in the world two weeks earlier than she was due, and yes, she was a bit small.

I rocked her in my arms. How had I managed to believe there could be a Wounded Baby Ward? And then it came to me: The blood and the pain, the naked life-and-death stakes of childbirth, had unearthed and exposed deep-buried memories of the Yom Kippur War. The anguish of war, I knew then, could never be erased from my heart—perhaps from the heart of any Israeli.

And yet . . . a moment later, as my newborn daughter Avigail nursed from my flowing breast, I forgot all about the war again, so enchanted was I by the glorious miracle of her life.

YEHUDA AMICHAI

FROM

Laments on
the War Dead

Is all this sorrow? I don't know,
I stood in the cemetery dressed
in the camouflage clothing of a live man, brown
pants and a shirt yellow as the sun.

Graveyards are cheap and unassuming.
Even the wastebaskets are too small to hold
the thin paper that wrapped the store-bought flowers.
Graveyards are disciplined, mannered things.
"I'll never forget you," reads
a small brick tablet in French,
I don't know who it is who won't forget
who's more unknown than the one who's dead.

Is all this sorrow? I think
so. "Be consoled in building the land." How
long can we build the land,
to gain in the terrible, three-sided
game of building, consolation, and death?
Yes, all this is sorrow. But
leave a little love always lit,
like the nightingale in a sleeping infant's room,
not that he knows what light is
and where it comes from, but it gives him
a bit of security and some silent love.

From Israeli Poetry: A Contemporary Anthology, *selected and translated by*
Warren Bargad and Stanley F. Chyet (Indiana University Press, 1986).

....

Yehuda Amichai is one of Israel's foremost writers. His poetry has been translated into more than twenty languages. Among his most recent works in translation is Selected Poetry, *translated by Chana Bloch and Stephen Mitchell (University of Berkeley, 1996), and* Open Closed Open, *translated by Chana Bloch and Chana Kronfeld (forthcoming from Harcourt, March 2000).*

TORQUEMADA

I am the Grand Inquisitor. My piercing Spanish eyes are wide with righteous indignation beneath my great black hood and cowl. I have the Jew in my grasp, but he refuses to recant. He assaults me with his spurious Hebrew logic. My mind storms at the sacrilege. I must restrain myself from wringing his neck like the chicken he resembles. Instead, I survey my armory of more persuasive implements and consider, with pleasure, which to use on this very special day: the tongs, the thumb screw, the rack, the fire. I sneeze.

This dungeon, my domain, is raw with winter. I can hear the wind rushing through the cracks between the enormous gray stones. Odors of mold and putrefaction are borne along like fish in the sea. Gusts find their way under my cassock, ripple my thighs like a horse's flanks. My arthritic fingers clutch Ecclesiastes to my chest, and I think that the Jew must suffer similar pangs without similar comfort. At least I am accustomed to this spiritual nether-world, while all he knows is his warm thatched cottage, homey with the moist heat and smell of his grandmother's soup. Not soon will he feast on beans and the blood of Christian children. Not soon will he escape the benevolent clutches of the Inquisition. I hold my lantern aloft to examine his fear, but when I sneeze again I drop it and the flame gutters and dies.

Despite the intense cold, I am sweating as I make my way down the darkened corridor. Is it the supernatural illumination that guides me through the pitch labyrinth beneath the castle which is burning me up from within or merely my hatred of the Jew? A fire out of control on a glacial slope, the extremes of temperature wrack and contort me to their whim. Tapping this bone this way and that bone that, they play upon my brittle spine like a musician. We undergo the same tortures, myself and the Jew, but it is a small price to pay for eternal salvation. Each howl of agony that drifts through the walls is bringing some lucky soul closer to God. I envy them. Then I feel it, an awesome winged presence in the corridor with me. A silent, dreadful, magnificent visitation. The Holy Ghost?

From somewhere in the midnight passage comes a void. "Who are you?"

"Your faithful servant," I reply, and drop to genuflect.

"I see no servant of the God of the Cross," the angry voice intones. "I see only . . . a Jew."

A Jew? "No, no, my Lord. Here," I tear at my hood, but where the black crest was in a knitted skullcap. "Here," I rip my shirt to reveal the crucifix ever upon my heart, but in place of the penitential hair-shirt is a flannel nightgown, and beneath it a star of David.

What a dream, what a terrible, frightening dream! I am back in my Toledo four-poster bed, Spanish lace hanging from its carved mahogany peaks. My red-cassocked junior brothers surround me, praying. Their voices are sweet, and far away, beneath my chamber, I can make out the restful undertone of the prisoners' cries. My court physician is in attendance, bending over me, peering intently through his gold-rimmed spectacles, attaching a leech to suck the fevered blood from my still pulsing forehead. I try to speak, but I have been too exhausted by me recent ordeal. Even now it is not over, and there is something wrong about these people I think I know so well. They are engaged in a hushed consultation, so I only hear fragments.

"A judgment."

"Raving since he got home."

". . . could have happened?"

Gradually their mellifluous Iberian accents become harsher, more guttural. Then their words themselves grow vague, then strange.

"On his way home from cheder."

"Church," I rasp to correct them.

"It was something the blacksmith's son said."

"The blackness. What the blackness said."

But they ignore me, so I scrutinize them. I catch a whiff of something fishy. My God, protect me, the court physician smells of herring! He is an imposter. I try to writhe from his insidious grip, but he and his aides hold me down. Sweat springs to my forehead, floods into my eyes, burns them with salt. I shut them against the pain and sight of the Jew.

It is not enough to banish the vision of treachery. Words come through, in Yiddish. Miraculously, I understand the infidel tongue. I reopen my eyes in wonder at their magic and in order to remember their faces on the day of retribution.

"Who was the last to see him?"

A man dressed as a schoolteacher answers, "The students all left together, but he ran ahead of the others. He often does."

"This wouldn't have happened if he were more friendly."

"So then Zevchik, the blacksmith's son, went up to him. There were words, then a fight."

"That Zevchik is a terror."

"Nonsense," a new voice declares. "When haven't young blacksmiths beat up young Jews? Zevchik is neither better nor worse than any Pole." This speaker's face is different from the others. It is less cared for but more caring. It is sensible, but it is also sensitive, and despite its lowly position on a straight-backed wooden chair in the corner it obviously commands a great deal of respect.

A mournful woman beside the chair sniffs, "He shouldn't fight." Her face is soft, madonnalike, haloed by a checkered handkerchief, but I will not allow myself to be seduced. It smells of soap and the other domestic chores of the faithless Jewish home.

The schoolteacher continues: "They were pulled apart, and he could hardly walk. Already he was crazy. So we brought him here, and he's been like this ever since."

The physician says: "I can find nothing drastically wrong with him. There are bruises but they're minor." He pulls the engorged slug off my forehead and drops it into a glass container, which he seals. "I don't usually advocate leeching, but in this case I thought there might be too much pressure on the brain. It will make him weak and light-headed, neither of which can hurt him more than his delirium."

Delirium, they say! Just because I can see through their pitiful masquerade they are desperate to convince me that I am mad. Endangered, yes, insane, never. I have fallen into the hands of Marranos, false converters, mockers of the sacrosanct baptismal ceremony. Pretending to be good Spaniards, they are merely cowards evading the snares of the Inquisition, secret Jews. I shall tear their disguises from them, strip them bare, flay them, burn them, and consecrate their ashes to the greater glory of Christ. "Jews!" I scream at them.

"Yes," the quiet man in the corner responds.

"Jews! Jews!" There is no worse insult.

"You are a Jew," he says.

"That's a filthy, degenerate lie. I was born to a sainted Christian woman, brought up in the household of the Lord, and have taken my place as the father of his earthly ministry . . . I am Torquemada."

Most everyone in the room blanches and starts back in horror. They cannot help but accord the truly righteous a certain esteem. I can see the effect my name has on all of them—except the one in the corner. He seems saddened but not fazed. He says, "Then Torquemada is a Jew."

I spring up and at his neck. My fingers are ten wriggling snakes reaching to sink their fangs through the soft flesh.

He does not move to defend himself. It is the other Jews who subdue me and tie me to the bed.

"A dybbuk," the mystic utters.

"No, a delirium," the rationalist maintains.

"Who," the woman hovering by the man in the corner pleads, "can help?"

First it is the doctor's turn. Besides leeching me he forces me to drink a vile liquid that tastes like tree bark. I feel it knotting my stomach, coursing through, and purging me from within. My pillow is drenched with sweat, but I will not succumb. When he lays hands on me, intruding on my privacy, I must endure the offense. Wrapped as securely as a baby in swaddling clothes,

I have only my words. "Do you not see the error of your ways, Jew? How dare you refuse to acknowledge the divinity of the one Lord above?"

As this is a matter for theology, the Rabbi steps in. He is an ugly, cantankerous old goat, a pious criminal. I can smell his beard and rank gabardine coat. I can smell the pungent reek of his faith, like rotting moss caught in a castle wind. "We are the ones who recognize the one Lord," he says. "It is you that divide him into three."

"The Trinity, most hallowed, most ineffable of mysteries. One in three, three in one. You cannot understand."

"Then how can we believe?"

"You claim to understand your Lord, Rabbi? A minor God he must certainly be."

The Rabbi steps warily about this bed that imprisons me, as if afraid that I might break loose. He explains, "No, we do not understand our Lord. His ways are beyond human comprehension. But we do know that he is One."

"As is mine," I tell him. "One in three, three in one. A mystery greater than yours. If there are two great mysteries, must not the greater be attributed to the greater God?"

The Rabbi tugs at his smelly beard, then replies, "Then why not one in five, five in one, one in a million, a million in one. The greater the mystery. . . ."

I have underestimated him. He has a point. Stalemate. I try another tack. "And the words of Christ on the cross?"

"Moses in the wilderness."

"Saint Paul."

"Elijah."

"Pope Innocent III."

"The Baal Shem Tov."

"We can banter religious authorities all night, Rabbi, but how can you deny the lay opinion of the citizens of the world? How can you deny their choice, which has given the community of Christ to be fruitful and multiply while you shrivel in this Polish backwater? How can you deny history?"

"Truth is not a matter of majority rule. How could we otherwise deny the words of the ancients as to the circulation of the blood, the roundness of the earth. A minority with truth on its side will always prevail, must always deny."

I am exasperated. I cannot contain myself. "Your minority is a rag-ridden, flea-bitten race of whorish, usurious, inbreeding Christ-killers and should be exterminated."

The Rabbi sighs, "No doubt if you have anything to say about it, we shall."

"Yes, I can see such a day, and not so long from now. It will be a splendid day, bathed in light and blood. There, on the white shore of the eternal kingdom, the good people shall be gathered. At sea, aboard a raft as large as an ark, the total remains of international Jewry are tied one to the other. The angels demand an end to the pestilence. I am proud to dip my torch to the scattered bundles of straw, which crackle and smoke until the oils of the wood and the sinews of the flesh catch fire. The flames mount. The last blasphemous prayers to a pagan God are drowned by the hosannas of the righteous Christian multitude as the final glorious auto-da-fé sinks sizzling beneath the waves. Rid forever of the Jewish contagion, it shall be a day of universal thanksgiving and universal belief in the one true God."

They are mute, agape before the power of my vision. Again, it is only the quiet man in the corner who can summon the will to speak to me. He asks calmly, "Are you a priest or a prophet?"

I could confound the doctor, refute the Rabbi, but this strange man's soft-spoken questions are beyond my ability to scorn. I can see the barks of my hands on his neck. I feel obligated to explain as best I can, and I do so with surprising modesty, in a voice almost like his. "It comes upon me at times."

The man merely nods. He puts a hand on the shoulder of the sobbing woman with the sweet face. "Go. Lie down," he advises her, and where the ministrations of the Rabbi and the potions of the doctor had failed to soothe her, his words have an inspirational effect. She nods and leaves, and I almost feel sympathy until I choke it back and remember that these are the killers of my Lord. Nursing dreams of revenge, I fall asleep.

When I wake, the man is still beside me, watching me.

"How did you sneak up on me, Jew?" I demand, and the man's eyelids shut and his head bows beneath their weight into his hands, as if my words were a magical incantation turning his flesh to stone. "I asked you a question, Jew. Now answer me. I say, 'Answer!'"

He moves no more than he has over the long course of the night.

"Answer me, dammit! Do you know who I am?"

In a weak, weary voice he moans, "Torquemada."

"Who?"

The man's head perks up, like a dog on its master's return from school, his eyes suddenly bright. Tentatively, hopefully, he asks, "You're not Torquemada?"

"What is this gibberish you keep repeating? Of course, I'm not," I say the alien name with distaste, "Torquemada!"

The man rises, arms outstretched as if to embrace me.

"I am Saladin, Caliph of Egypt, Armenia, Mesopotamia, and Palestine, Ruler of the East and Representative of Allah."

The man collapses in a heap at the foot of the decadent Western bedpiece I am confined to. I would prefer a straw pallet on a baked mud floor to this frivolous, womanly cushion, shackles to the leather tongs that coddle as they bind me, the dungeons of Christ to this Jewish notion of luxurious imprisonment.

The woman with the sad face comes rushing to the aid of the man on the floor. Kneeling beside him, she turns to me, and cries, "What have you done to him, you ungrateful child? What have you done to yourself?"

"I do nothing for myself. My life is in the service of Allah."

The Rabbi, newly entered with pie crumbs upon his beard, looks as if I have just condemned him to decapitation. "Why do you do this?" he whines.

The man on the floor whispers, "Leave him be." This is a curious type of charity he practices. Notwithstanding his moment of weakness, I have the feeling that he is the only one who is a worthy antagonist.

"What has happened to you?" I ask him. "We were born together in the desert of the patriarch Abraham. We are cousins, yet you have left our common inheritance. Your faces are white from lack of the nourishing sun. You have no strength, no stamina. You are no better than Christians."

He seems staggered by my accusation, but before he can respond I continue: "Look about you. A cottage instead of a tent, an oven instead of an open fire." At the mention of warmth of the European cold comes through the walls to freeze me. "Look at this feather quilt," I chatter, "and the worst of it is that it may be necessary in this godforsaken climate. You may have managed to capture me, but you are the ones who are prisoners in your comfortable homes."

I strain against my bonds, but I no longer have the power to resist them. I am betrayed by my own muscles, which have sunk into and become as one with the jelly of the mattress. The color is draining from my face, and the extra flesh shrinking from the head of my penis. Circumcision is the last indignity; I am becoming Jewish, and I cannot stand it. They are everything I despise. They are feeble and overintellectual, servile, cultish. They smell of the shop and the shul. Every one of them is as prematurely old as their race.

I think that we are born with our thoughts already dwelling in our brains. Try as we may to consider other points of view, we always return to the place where we started. I know in my blood that I must kill Jews, and that is all there is to that. We are family, but there are no more bitter hatreds than those among relations. Yes, there are reasons for this eternal enmity, their stubborn refusal to acknowledge the one true prophet, Mohammed, their pious stance that makes the rest of us feel like dirt, their ugly habits, their evil nature; but as sufficient as all this may be, it is also superfluous. The main reason Jews must be killed is tautological, because they must be killed.

As if he can read my mind, the solitary man still on the floor asks a simple question, "And what will the world be like when you have killed all of us?"

The answer is so simple I cannot understand how he does not see it. "Why, it will be like a world without Jews."

The man nods sagely and returns to the chair to resume his vigil.

Night and day the man stays with me as I sleep to the fevered dreams of Judaism and wake to the might and glory of Jew-haters everywhere. I am Pharaoh, watching the pyramids rise on the mixture of limestone bricks and Hebrew sweat. I am Nebuchadnezzar sacking Jerusalem. I am Herod and I am Haman. I am Persian, Roman, Briton, and Turk. I am every prince or pope who has ever stoned or hung, drowned or burned the Chosen People. I am the proud persecutor ranging through the millennia, searching out my victims wherever they hide, for the taint of their blood always gives them away. The despised race always dies, but they always survive as a remnant that troubles my dreams.

The doctor and the rabbi must admit that I am too powerful for their meager talents to deal with, but given their one-track minds, they can only think to call in other doctors and rabbis. These celebrated men in three-piece suits and silver-rimmed pincenez jab needles into me, infecting and extracting various vital fluids. They recommend diets and physical regimens. They mumble words of prayer and parade Torahs before me as though I were a sacrificial goat. They confront me with alleged teachers and neighbors and pallid bookworms whom they claim are the companions of the imaginary childhood they have constructed for me. One wants to beat me, saying, "A good switching is all he needs," while another dangles a gold watch idiotically back and forth in front of me. Whatever their remedy for whatever Semitic disorder they have attributed to me instead of themselves, they are equally flawed by their bad blood and incapable of effecting any change in me.

The only one I have a hard time with is the man in the corner, who, as far as I can tell, never leaves the room. It is small compensation that the rabbis also seem to have problems with this contemplative statue of a man. When urged to some violent action by one of his failed wonder-workers, he answers with a definitive incongruity that will brook no response, "The boy always had a good imagination."

Second only to the man is the woman who is frequently brought in and out of my cell, where she sobs, the self-made martyr of some private tragedy. Still, when one of her washerwoman companions makes a snide remark about me, the woman reins in her sorrow and answers, "At least he's eating."

Suddenly I have an idea. I understand why this couple does not disturb me as much as the others. They too are prisoners. She was my chambermaid, he perhaps an aged retainer. Now I have a plan. I bide my time, and when I am alone with them I whisper, "Listen, I know who you really are, and I know that you know who I really am, so help me escape. I will reward you with half of my kingdom."

But the man only mutters, "And I would reward you with my entire kingdom," and again we all lapse into a silence as deep as the ocean.

The woman's long-drawn-out sigh is like a bubble floating from the depths to break at the surface of that ocean. "I don't know," she says. "I just don't know where to turn." A hysterical note comes into her voice, and she yearns to leap. "We've had every Jew between here and Warsaw here, and none of them can help. What can we do?"

"Wait for the Lord, blessed be He," the man reassures her, but despite himself he raises his eyes, entreating his Lord to stop taking his own sweet holy time and grant deliverance now. There is an ominous rumbling in the skies; the room grows dim. A ray of light pierces the dusk like a spear. It is as if the desired redemption has indeed come down from the heavens and struck the man between the eyes. He asks the woman to repeat herself.

She is baffled and hesitant. "I don't know where to turn?" she says phrase by halting phrase, like a youthful violinist. "I just don't know where to turn?"

"Yes. Yes. Go on."

"We've had every doctor and Rabbi and teacher and ev—"

"No," he cuts her off, "that isn't what you said." He has a strange wakeful gleam in his eye, like someone with a present hidden behind his back. "You said that we've had every Jew here."

She begins to look at him with the same concern that has so far been reserved for me. Warily, she asks, "So who else is there?"

"There are 'his' people."

"Goyim?" The word escapes with horror.

"One in particular . . . the Zevchik lad."

"The one who did this? No, no, I forbid it. You must be crazy too. No. Absolutely not."

"He can't have any worse reaction to Zevchik than he has to us. We have to."

A sallow, pimply youth is brought into my cell between the rabbi and the doctor. "You," I call to him. "Boots!"

He cringes, but he does not obey.

"Are you deaf, boy? I said that I wanted my boots, and I meant now. So shine them, wax them, buff them, and bring them before I have you spitted like a pig. . . . Don't just stair, and while you're about your task, bring my waistcoat, and also my saber, then saddle my horse. The time has come, don't you hear me, the time has come for action. Come on, snap to it! I don't have to tell you why this is necessary. They poison our wells. They steal children like yourself to make their filthy matzos. They have fortunes hidden to seduce our maidens, subvert our morals, and corrupt our race, these Rothschilds.

"But we won't let them. The international Jewish conspiracy must be smashed. It must be rooted out of the high places it has usurped and the low places in which it breeds. We shall start a pogrom that will inspire good men everywhere. God's cavalry shall charge out of the steppes into the *shtetls*, and raze them flat. Get my boots, boy, for today, in the name of our Holy Father the Tsar and dear Mother Russia, today, against the Jews, today shall ride Chmielnicki, the king of the Cossacks!"

The boy turns on his heel, but the man from the corner has risen in stealth and stands behind him like a wall. "Now tell me, son, exactly what happened between you."

"Don't say a word," I order.

"Don't be afraid," the man says, "and please don't be ashamed. We mean you no harm. You see we must find out what happened, and you're the only one who can tell us."

"Silence!" I am frightened as by none of the previous torturers. "Silence, I command you, silence, you peasant!"

"I cursed him," the boy mutters. "I called him a dirty Jew."

"Who are you calling a Jew?"

"Please go on."

"I said other things . . . I'm not sure. Whatever came to my mind. We always do. It's what we always do." His audience rapt, the boy becomes positively voluble. If I could I would strangle him, but I am trapped and gnash my teeth fruitlessly. "Oh, he was a strange one," the boy says. "He actually asked me why I hated Jews. Then when I answered him we started fighting."

The calm voice makes one last query, "And what did you say?"

"I said it was a stupid question. I told him that he knew why we hate you . . . because you hate yourselves."

The boy chatters on, and the rabbis exchange views on this new profanity, but an overpowering silence emanates from the man. He ushers the boy to the door and nods good-bye to the rabbis. He seems to sleepwalk to my bed, and for the first time during my captivity I am afraid he may harm me. His expression wavers unnaturally, still it is his usual mournful tone that repeats to me, "because we hate ourselves."

I blurt out, "Because your God hates you."

"Why?"

"You need to ask why? Because of me, Chmielnicki, and because of Herod and Haman, and because of Torquemada. Or will you tell me that's how He shows His love?"

And I start to cry. I press my eyes shut, but the tears well up and squeeze through. I hold my breath, but sniffles choke me and I must gasp for air. I am a dam, leaking, cracking, crumbling, and with each tear I feel my ability to resist failing. My years seep away, and with each tear a Jewishness rises in me, and the more it grows the stronger it gets. Samson wasn't a Jew until Delilah cut his hair. The dam bursts, and the torrential flow of Jewish lamentation sweeps me out to sea, to drown if need be with the rest of my people. My power gone, I succumb to the pathetic traits of my race with a rush of pure joy. I am sobbing uncontrollably now, because I think that if He doesn't cry of us, someone has to, and it might as well be me.

"It's all right. It's all right now," the man with me repeats over and over again, working swiftly to untie the straps that hold me down, hugging me as I spring up. His arms around me are just as strong as but so much more secure than the straps, and his voice is understanding and wise and loving. "It's all OK. Maybe the Messiah's been a little late, maybe he'll be a little later, but Torquemada's gone, and we don't have to worry. We have each other and it's the twentieth century of civilized man. There, there. What harm could possibly come to us in 1928?"

Between sobs I manage to gulp, "Yes, Daddy."

Melvin J. Bukiet is the author of Signs and Wonders *(Picador, 1999),* After *(St. Martin's Press, 1996), and* While the Messiah Tarries *(Harvest Books, 1995). "Torquemada" is included in his collection* Stories of an Imaginary Childhood *(Northwestern University Press, 1992). He also edited* Neurotica: Jewish Writers on Sex *(Norton, 1999).*

Zusia

Lying on his deathbed, Rabbi Zusia was surrounded by his devoted disciples. Suddenly his eyes opened wide and a look of great anguish flickered on his face.

"Rebbe, rebbe, what is the matter?" his disciples cried.

"I dreamed that I came before the throne of the Almighty," Zusia replied, in a stricken voice. "The Holy One did not say to me, 'Zusia! Why were you not Moses?' And he did not say to me, 'Zusia! Why were you not Jacob?' And he did not say to me, 'Why were you not the prophet Isaiah?'"

The Rebbe looked piercingly into the eyes of his disciples. "What the Almighty said was, 'Zusia! Why were you not Zusia?'"

A Ride with Fonda

The day I turned twenty-six, I found myself by sheer coincidence in the back of a black limousine in Tel Aviv sitting next to Jane Fonda.

Fonda was talking. Not about Sinatra or Bogart or Dietrich or Gable; not about her own successes, even though they hovered about her like an aura. Fonda was talking about someone named Rukhama Sasson, but since it was hard for her to pronounce the guttural "kh," the woman's name came out "Ruhama." As she spoke, her public face seemed to crack along tiny fault lines.

Well, said Fonda, Rukhama Sasson was a woman of sixty or so—Fonda had known her from back home. Rukhama was liberated from Dachau when she was twenty. A year later she married, and she and her husband immigrated to Israel together. For the next forty years, her life seemed to glide by—she raised her four children, set her house in order, her children had children. The past seemed to have been forgotten. A happy ending. A picture-perfect story.

Rukhama's husband made a lot of money, Fonda went on, and the Sassons were sent to America as emissaries of the state they had helped to build. With their sons and daughters and three grandchildren staying behind, Rukhama was finally free of the demands of everyday life. She was an affluent woman of leisure ready to discover the ends of the earth. But it was precisely then that the images she had sealed off so long ago began to bubble to the surface. The nightmares started.

She really had *not* remembered. She had seen none of the films. On certain days of the year back in Israel she had refused to turn on the television or radio. When her children used to ask why, she would respond, "I wiped it out."

But living in a foreign country now, her nights had become such torment that she sought out a healer to restore her sleep.

"She was too terrified to close her eyes," said Fonda. I felt an inescapable undercurrent seeping into her voice.

"How could such heavy old memories come up after so many years?" she asked.

I turned to her, a meticulously put-together, elegant woman entirely strange to me, and finally opened my mouth. "Rukhama Sasson could be *my* mother," I said softly.

"My mother turned off the television and radio on certain days of the year in Israel too . . . but her pain never went away, never disappeared. Her pain had floated into her amniotic fluid. We, her children, drank it in her milk. To this day I can still hear her lamenting, 'Maybe I never should have brought you into the world. Maybe I sinned giving birth to you.'"

But as I spoke now, I felt as if I were hugging my mother, as if now, finally, I was old enough to hug her. Mama, I heard myself silently saying, I inherited the scent of death from you, maybe in your milk, maybe in your blood, maybe in a dream, maybe in your screams in the middle of the night all through the 1950s. Like fibers that hang suspended in the air, pulling and twisting. . .

"My mother never talks of her childhood," I went on. "It's as if her life before the war belonged to someone else, as if it is split in half by an unbreachable chasm."

Fonda listened like a taut string.

"Israel is full of Rukhama Sassons who beg for forgiveness because the stain of blood and the smell of ashes from their own tormented past have clung to their sons and their daughters."

Fonda shut the window of the black limousine and stared outside. She was silent and so was I. And then, suddenly, I recalled that Fonda's mother had slashed her own wrists.

Fonda pinched her dry hands together. With the stain of blood and smell of ashes hovering in the air, we did not look at one another again.

Translated by Miriyam Glazer

Nava Semel

Israeli writer Nava Semel has written fiction, plays, scripts, and librettos. She won the National Jewish Book Award for Becoming Gershona *(Viking, 1990) and the Prime Minister of Israel's Award for Literature. She writes often of the influence of the Holocaust on the second-generation. Her story, "Hunger," is featured in* Dreaming the Actual: Contemporary Fiction and Poetry by Israeli Women Writers *(State University of New York Press, 2000).*

Di yerushe/The Legacy:

A Parable About History and Bob-mayses, Barszcz, and Borsht and the Future of the Jewish Past

This is no *bobe-mayse.** I never knew my grandmothers, both of whom died in the war, and it's only recently that I've gotten even a glimpse of what my bobes might have been like by watching my eighty-one-year-old mother, Mamo Lo. Oddly enough I, too, thought childless, am experiencing a state of *bobe*-hood. More and more, Mama Lo and I are sharing the aches and pains of getting old and older and bridging our lifelong generation gap. Who would have thought? But then these are peculiar times.

For example, lately Mama Lo has been instructing me about "when the time comes . . ." and showing me the desk drawer with her living will and the jewelry box with Elza's watch, not especially valuable, but the only physical link to my twenty-four-year-old almost-sister who committed suicide over thirty years ago. Occasionally she walks me through the apartment, pointing to this or that. Sometimes she stares at her well-stocked bookcases of Ringelblum, Levi, Charlotte, Herman Wouk, Howard Fast, and Jane Austen and George Eliot, at the framed reproductions of Chagall and Van Gogh, and at the *tshatshkes* of kittens, vases, miniature musicians (many of them presents from me). In a gesture of puzzlement (perhaps despair), she throws up her hands: "What are you going to do with . . . ?" she begins, then stops and changes the subject with a shrug.

Though she has experienced two world wars, poverty, and serious illnesses, I suspect Mama Lo is admitting to herself for the first time that she has no choice but to accept her lack of control over her own life and mine. Knowing my forgetfulness and essential anarchism, she cannot feel easy about passing on the pots of sturdy jades and blossoming African violets. Actually, I'm not certain what she feels because I have no idea what it is like to be eighty-one, and also because, with iron-clad tenacity, Mama Lo has kept her inner life a locked vault. It is a vault to which she is not about to bequeath me the key—History be damned, she is saying—What is private is private.

So these days we are both silent about what we both know: that at some point, I will take possession of her possessions, dismantle her apartment, and, barring catastrophe, continue with my life for possibly two or three decades without her. In other words, my life as a daughter will come to an abrupt end and I will cease being Mama Lo and her generation's future and be transformed into a true *bobe*, the next generation's past.

Theoretically, legacies and inheritances are simple: some things we accept and keep, even if with great sadness; others we discard because they're inconvenient, useless, simply passé. A watch like Elza's—orphan child-survivor, dreaming poet, determined suicide—embodies so much public and private history that I've never been able to claim it for myself. So when the time comes, the watch will be transferred to my desk drawer. But I am determined eventually to bequeath it to someone, someone younger—not a relative, because I have none—but someone to whom its fierce and painful history will be important, and whose arm will display it like an honor, rather than a wound.

Mama Lo's other bequests will be more problematic. Should I, for example, keep a leaky pot—its white enamel worn, its rim dented— but Mama Lo's (and my own) sole physical link to Poland (postwar, of course, but Poland nevertheless)? What historical purpose will it serve standing on a shelf behind my teflon pans, my well-used wok and bamboo steamers? Does such a pot belong in a museum and should I try to donate it? ("It's the very pot in which Mama Lo cooked her *borscht*—on *both* sides of the Atlantic. Believe me it tells the quintessential twentieth-century Jewish story.")

And then there's the album with photographs of people I don't quite remember: a man and woman standing by the white brick oven in our Lodz apartment or a teenager kneeling by a sandbox in a park—ordinary people who, because of their imagination, stupidity and/or luck, just happened to survive. Should I ask Mama Lo to name them? I've no family, so what does it matter? Won't such an album inevitably end up in some collectibles barn in Columbia County in upstate New York to be browsed through by eager weekenders trying to furnish their newly built A-frame with an aura of history? On the other hand, the album is part of *my life, my past*—one which my aging brain has increasingly more trouble retaining, a past which, I confess, I've already distilled (or thinned—depending on your point of view) as I've tried to "get on" with my life.

The truth is that for most of my adulthood I've been braced against Mama Lo's disapproval, conscious I did not fulfill her wish and emulate her and her one-bedroom apartment in a three-bedroom one of my own, fully furnished with a husband and children. Instead, I went off and settled into a wall-less, closet-less loft which I share with another woman who has no legal relationship to me, but with whom I also share my life.

Yet, for all my rebelliousness and alternativity, a part of my identity—the *Jewish* part—has been inextricably intertwined with Mama Lo and the life of her generation. *My* vaulted secret is that I've been a dependent Jew—dependent on Mama Lo's generation to provide me with a sense of *hemshekh*/continuity. They've been the visible *goldene keyt*/the golden chain to which I've wanted to hook the link I've been forging through my life and my work. With them gone, where am I supposed to hang myself?

To put it another way: *Vos iz geshikhte?*/What is history and what is my place in it? And how is time defined with any accuracy by human events? The Middle Ages. The Renaissance. The Age of

Reason. How do we know when one age ends and another begins? I wonder with increasing urgency as I ready myself to begin the Jewish generation relay race in which I've been entered.

Take *borscht*, for example. Consider that beets were unknown to us at the time of the destruction of the Temple and were not among the hastily packed foods our *bobes* took into Babylon or later into the northwestern *goles*/exile. Then consider the centrality of borscht in modern Eastern European Jewish culture. By what process did this essential component of Jewish life emerge?

Borscht entered Jewish life many centuries ago—through the kitchen. The first Jewish mention of beets, I believe, occurs in *A bobe, an eydes / A Grandmother, A Witness*, a recently discovered collection that is bound to rival Glickl's *Memoirs*. Among its many fragmentary stories, *A bobe, an eydes* contains a series of tributes to a certain Gitl *bas* Frume *di frume** who, according to one *bobe mayse*, lived in the later part of the thirteenth century in the town of Knin. Knin was far from her ancestors' beloved Ashkenaz, very far east, in fact, in a region we nostalgically remember today as *poyln*/Poland—the cradle of *yidishkayt, der yidisher oyster*/the Jewish treasure—but where, in Gitl's time, the buds of *yidishe geshikhte im kultur*/history and culture were barely formed, much less beginning to bloom.

It was some time during that Yiddish dawn that Gitl *bas* Frume *di frume* forged a secret friendship with Grushenka, even though Janek, Grushenka's brother, beat up Yankl, Gitl's brother, on a regular basis. One Sunday morning after sneaking out of church, Grushenka led Gitl (without Frume's knowledge) into her mother's Christian kitchen, where, for the first time, Gitl smelled the sweet, dark aroma of *barszcz*. "*Treyf!*" *undzere yidishe tokhter*/our young Jewish girl declared that night to her younger sister Chava, thereby conveying her understanding of the nature of the soup's bones and, indeed, its entire culinary context. But then, much to her sister's horror, Gitl added with *emesdike benkshaft*/heartfelt longing: "*Ober es shmekt azoy gut!*/But it smells so good!"

Like other texts whose authors were neither official recorders nor note takers, but ordinary homemakers focused more on an event's ingredients than on its development and denouement, *A bobe, an eydes* gives scant information about the process of Judaization of the Polish *barszcz*. Perhaps once, perhaps more than once, the girl tasted the forbidden friend's forbidden food. In any case, at some point, after numerous visits and sniffs, much finger-pointing at the market place, two or three public tantrums, and repeated posings of the proverbial *"Ober, far vos nisht?/*Why not?"—the impetus behind all creative leaps—Gitl convinced Frume *di frume* to act: (*"Dos meydl makht mir in gantsn meshige. Tog un nakht redt zi bloyz fun* buraki *un* barszcz!/The girl's driving me completely mad. Day and night she talks only of *buraki* and *barszcz!"*) And so the frazzled mother peeled the bleeding vegetables into a pot of boiling water, added some *beyner, tsiker, knobl, un tsibeles/*bones, sugar, garlic and onions and, through trial and error—*tsu gedikht, tsu shiter, tsu zis, tsu zoyer/*too thick, too thin, too sweet, too tart—the soup looked, tasted, and smelled exactly like the *barszcz* in Grushenka's mother's kitchen with the added advantage it could pass rabbinic inspection: *s'iz geven kusher/*it was kosher.

The rest *iz poshet/*is simple. By the first decade of the fifteenth century when Gitl's great-granddaughter, Frume *di freylekhe,** was already a married *baleboste/*homemaker, the Slavic-rooted *barszcz* had become *borsht*, the Yiddish word for the quintessential Jewish soup.

Given such history, it is not surprising that today, near the end of the twentieth century, I am preoccupied with leaky pots, with Elza's watch (which, despite being idle for almost thirty years, began ticking the second I wound it), with photo albums, and with the survival of *borscht* itself in Jewish kitchens dominated by woks and bamboo steamers. Nor is it surprising that I am preoccupied with Mama Lo's entire *yerushe*, including everything she lost almost sixty years ago so that when she debarked in *di goldene medine/*the golden land, Mama Lo had nothing but a goosedown *koldra* (which a year later caught fire from a faulty heating pad), some crumbling photographs, a pot purchased in Lodz shortly after liberation—and me. That year *poyln* was no longer a blooming garden, but a country-sized wall-less graveyard and Mama Lo's past a *vistenish/*a void, something that history and nature abhor and immediately engulf, thereby allowing the transformation of alien weeds into beloved indigenous flowers and a *treyf barszcz* into the embodiment of a *kushere heym.*

So when the time comes, I will have no choice. Somehow I will find my place on the historical continuum and try to observe and take notes. I will go to Sally and Linda's seder and recline on the Moroccan, Israeli, and Native American rugs. Together we will retell the ancient story as it was passed from *bobe* to *bobe* and read from our xeroxed *hagadahs* decorated with images of ancient goddesses and interspersed with the texts of witches' incantations, peace songs between Hagar and Sarah, tributes to midwives, toasts to the liberation of Palestinians, and praisesongs and poems to Hannah Senesh, Yokheved, and Gitl *bas* Frume *di frume.* At appropriate moments, my women friends and I will raise our cups of grape juice and greet Miriam the Prophetess, drink the vegetarian chicken soup, dunk the parsley in the bitter waters, chew the symbolic mortar, and burn the sweet-scented incense. Each year we will substitute this for that and add that to this and sing and chant recalling the tears and losses and recite (in English, of course) "*hayntiks yor knekht, dos kumendike yor fraye froyen*/this year we are slaves, next year liberated women." And a few years from now, sometime around the year 2000, we will feel familiar, comforted, and grounded in our tradition and look back upon the seders of our childhoods as the ancient ceremonies of another century and era— which is exactly what they will have become.

But until then, I am at Mama Lo's service. Whenever she wants to recall more vividly the *poyln fun ire kinderyorn*/Poland of her childhood and the sweetness of my *bobe* Rikla's *kikh*, a kitchen whose ashes and dust are now indistinguishable from those of the Second Temple—I will take Mama Lo to Second Avenue and Teresa's Polish Café and order *borscht*, the same *treyf barszcz* Gitl *bas* Frume *di frume* first smelled in Grushenka's mother's kitchen. As Mama Lo and I breathe in its dark, rich aroma, we will begin talking for the first time *bobe tsu bobe* about the miracles of our common past and the mystery of our separate futures.

....

Irena Klepfisz is the author of A Few Words in the Mother Tongue *(poetry) and* Dreams of an Insomniac *(essays). She has translated and written extensively on Yiddish women writers, including a feminist introduction to the groundbreaking anthology* Found Treasures: Stories by Yiddish Women Writers. *She serves as an editorial consultant for Yiddish language and literature and as Chair of the Advisory Board of the Jewish feminist journal* Bridges. *She teaches Jewish Women's Studies at Barnard College. This story first appeared in* Prairie Schooner.

Hovering Above the Pit

It was a dark, cold night in the Janowska road camp.* Suddenly, a stentorian shout pierced the air: "You are all to evacuate the barracks immediately and report to the vacant lot. Anyone remaining inside will be shot on the spot!"

Pandemonium broke out in the barracks. People pushed their way to the doors while screaming the names of friends and relatives. In a panic-stricken stampede, the prisoners ran in the direction of the big open field.

Exhausted, trying to catch their breath, they reached the field. In the middle were two huge pits.

Suddenly, with their last drop of energy, the inmates realized where they were rushing, on that cursed dark night in Janowska.

Once more, the cold, healthy voice roared in the night: "Each of you dogs who values his miserable life and wants to cling to it must jump over one of the pits and land on the other side. Those who miss will get what they rightfully deserve—ra-ta-ta-ta-ta."

Imitating the sound of a machine gun, the voice trailed off into the night followed by a wild, coarse laughter. It was clear to the inmates that they would all end up in the pits. Even at the best of times it would have been impossible to jump over them, all the more so on that cold, dark night in Janowska. The prisoners standing at the edge of the pits were skeletons, feverish from disease and starvation, exhausted from slave labor and sleepless nights. Though the challenge that had been given them was a matter of life and death, they knew that for the S.S. and the Ukrainian guards it was merely another devilish game.

Among the thousands of Jews on that field in Janowska was the rabbi of Bluzhov, Rabbi Israel Spira. He was standing with a friend, a freethinker from a large Polish town whom the rabbi had met in the camp. A deep friendship had developed between the two.

"Spira, all of our efforts to jump over the pits are in vain. We only entertain the Germans and their collaborators, the Askaris. Let's sit down in the pits and wait for the bullets to end our wretched existence," said the friend to the rabbi.

"My friend," said the rabbi, as they were walking in the direction of the pits, "man must obey the will of God. If it was decreed from heaven that pits be dug and we be commanded to jump, pits will be dug and jump we must. And if, God forbid, we fail and fall into the pits, we will reach the World of Truth a second later, after our attempt. So, my friend, we must jump."

The rabbi and his friend were nearing the edge of the pits; the pits were rapidly filling up with bodies.

The rabbi glanced down at his feet, the swollen feet of a fifty-three-year-old Jew ridden with starvation and disease. He looked at his young friend, a skeleton with burning eyes.

As they reached the pit, the rabbi closed his eyes and commanded in a powerful whisper, "We are jumping!" When they opened their eyes, they found themselves standing on the other side of the pit.

"Spira, we are here, we are here, we are alive!" the friend repeated over and over again, while warm tears streamed from his eyes. "Spira, for your sake, I am alive; indeed, there must be a God in heaven. Tell me, Rebbe, how did you do it?"

"I was holding on to my ancestral merit. I was holding on to the coattails of my father, and my grandfather and my great-grandfather, of blessed memory," said the rabbi and his eyes searched the black skies above. "Tell me, my friend, how did *you* reach the other side of the pit?"

"I was holding on to you," replied the rabbi's friend.

*Janowska Road Camp, established in 1941, was situated near the cemeteries and sand mountains outside the city of Lvov, in the Ukraine. Officially a forced-labor camp, it was in reality a place of torture and death, notorious for the cruelty of its German commanders and their Ukrainian and Russian collaborators. In many instances, inmates were brutally murdered for the entertainment of the camp officials. Tens of thousands of Jews met their deaths there.

Yaffa Eliach

Based on a conversation of the Grand Rabbi of Bluzhov, Rabbi Israel Spira, with Baruch Singer, January 3, 1975. Yaffa Eliach is the founder of the first Center for Holocaust Documentation and Research in the United States, and the author of Hasidic Tales of the Holocaust *(Avon, 1982), and the new* There Once Was a World: A 900-Year Chronicle of the Shtetl of Eishyshok *(Little, Brown, & Co., 1998).*

İn Days Gone By and İn Our Own Time

S.B. Unsdorfer spent much of the second World War in concentration camps. In the camp of Neider-Orschel, he kept a diary in which he entered the Hebrew dates and festivals. One day in December 1943 he discovered that Hanukkah was only a few days off. To boost the morale of his fellow prisoners, he decided to kindle some kind of light for the festival occasion.

They knew, of course, that Jewish law did not compel them to risk their lives to fulfill a commandment. But they were in such great spiritual and physical distress that they wanted to rise above the misery of their situation, to imbue it with the heroic spirit of their ancestors. They wanted to warm their starving souls and inspire them with the hope, faith, and courage to keep going through the long, grim, and icy winter.

The main difficulty—as during the first Hanukkah—was to obtain some of the precious oil in the first place. One of these latter-day Maccabees convinced the work superintendent that his machine would work better if it were oiled regularly every morning. The work superintendent approved, and they arranged to keep a small can of fine machine oil in the toolbox to which the conspirators had access.

On Monday evening after roll call, while everyone was having their long-awaited meager portion of hot but tasteless soup, Unsdorfer busied himself under his bunk preparing a menorah. He put some oil in the empty half of a shoe polish tin and made a wick out of a few threads from his thin blanket. When everything was ready, he quickly joined the table to eat his dinner before inviting all his friends to the ceremony. Suddenly, as he was sipping his soup, he realized that they had forgotten matches.

Hungry as they were, everyone was ordered to leave a little soup, which was then bartered in the next room for a cigarette. This was presented to Joseph the chef, in exchange for a box of matches, with no questions asked.

After dinner, Unsdorfer made the blessings over the tiny makeshift menorah. The inmates of the camp crowded around the flickering flame and joined in the singing. In the small flame, the inmates could see images of their lost homes, of their vanished parents, brothers, sisters, wives, children.

A roar of *Achtung* shocked them back to their reality. The Nazi sublieutenant and his Alsatian hound were making one of their surprise visits. He sniffed suspiciously; he had smelled the oil.

The little Hanukkah light flickered on the ground as the Nazi and his dog began to parade along the bunks toward them. The nearer he came the more the Jews began to lose hope. Suddenly, sirens began to wail, signaling an air raid in progress. Within seconds all lights in the camp were switched off automatically. Unsdorfer was able to put out the Hanukkah candle.

This was the sign, he said, the miracle of Hanukkah, the recognition of our struggle:

Outside in the ice-cold, star-studded night, with the heavy drone of Allied bombers over our heads, I kept on muttering the traditional blessing to the God who wrought miracles for His people in days gone by and in our own time.

....

Adapted from Freema Gottlieb, The Lamp of God: A Jewish Book of Light *(Jason Aronson, 1989), and S.B. Unsdorfer,* The Yellow Star *(Thomas Yoseloff, 1961).*

THE MIRACLE OF HANUKKAH

According to tradition, the miracle of Hanukkah was that, when the Maccabees sought to rekindle the Temple menorah, the very little oil they were able to find lasted an unexpected eight days. But the real miracle is that they went ahead and lit the menorah on the *first* day, even though they did not know what the next day would bring.

It is that same miracle that enabled the Jews to endure through every generation and every exile. For had we been discouraged by our anxieties about the future, we would have long since lost the capacity to survive.

....

Adapted from Eliyahu Kitov, The Book of Our Heritage *(Jerusalem, 1968).*

PLAYING WITH
THREE STRINGS

We have seen Yitzhak Perlman
Who walks the stage with braces on both legs,
On two crutches.

He takes his seat, unhinges the clasps of his legs,
Tucking one leg back, extending the other,
Laying down his crutches, placing the violin under his chin.

On one occasion one of his violin strings broke.
The audience grew silent but the violinist did not leave the stage.
He signaled the maestro, and the orchestra began its part.
The violinist played with power and intensity on only three strings.

With three strings, he modulated, changed and
Recomposed the piece in his head
He retuned the strings to get different sounds,
Turned them upward and downward.

The audience screamed delight,
Applauded their appreciation.
Asked later how he had accomplished this feat,
The violinist answered
It is my task to make music with what remains.

A legacy mightier than a concert.
Make music with what remains.
Complete the song left for us to sing,
Transcend the loss,
Play it out with heart, soul, and might
With all remaining strength within us.

Harold M. Schulweis is a rabbi at Valley Beth Shalom in Encino, California. He is founder of the Jewish Foundation for the Righteous and the author of For Those Who Can't Believe *(HarperCollins, 1994).*

A Plane Truth

Yaakov, a seventh-grade student in a yeshiva in Brooklyn, was an orphan who lived with his grandmother. His young mother had passed away two years before, while the family was still in Russia. After coming to America, his father married a woman unwilling to raise the child, so Yaakov was sent to live with his aged grandmother, who spoke no English.

Yaakov was a brilliant student. Although he had received no Jewish education in Russia, before long he was the top student in his grade at the yeshiva. His teacher had merely to recite a passage of Talmud once, and Yaakov could repeat it verbatim. His comprehension was nothing short of astounding; often he would ask the very questions raised by the earliest commentators, the *Rishonim*.

But there was a problem. Yaakov had a penchant for making intricate paper planes and flicking them across the classroom. His classmates thought he was hysterically clever, but the planes infuriated his rebbes and teachers. He would build a squadron of tiny planes, set them up on his desk, and propel them one by one on missions all over the classroom.

Nothing that any teacher—or even the principal—said to Yaakov had any effect on his behavior. He knew the material, he achieved high grades—but his planes took off and landed on a regular basis. Since Yaakov's grandmother could not speak English, his late mother's sister and her husband were summoned to school on Parents' Night to speak with the Rebbe.

The Rebbe took out a few of the small planes from his desk. "Yaakov is a very bright boy," he began. "His mind is as sharp as any I have ever seen for a seventh grader. But he is always playing with these planes, shooting them all around the class. I like him. He's a good boy. But he is very disruptive, and won't stop no matter what I say."

Yaakov's aunt picked up one of the planes, turning it slowly and examining its intricacy. Suddenly she began to cry softly.

"What's wrong?" asked the shocked Rebbe.

"My sister, his mother, taught him to make these planes when he was a little boy," she said.

Now the Rebbe understood his orphaned student. In Yaakov's uncertain voyage toward the future, he was clinging to the memory of his past.

Adapted from "It was Plane and Simple" from Paysach J. Krohn's collection Echoes of the Maggid: Heartwarming Stories and Parables of Wisdom and Inspiration *(Mesorah Publications, 1999). Rabbi Krohn is a fifth-generation mohel (ritual circumciser) and the author of five collections of inspirational stories.*

Song

My brother phones. "She is settling into a coma."

He has visited our mother in the nursing home.

"She has received good care," he says, and tells me about a burly Chicano who tried to coax our mother to eat.

"'Mama,' the hospital worker said, 'Just a little soup? A little Jell-O?'"

"But she doesn't have the strength to sip through a straw," says my brother.

Her body is disobedient to its training and its history. Eyes will not focus; legs refuse to stand; the heart will not do its job. For the past two weeks she has been wearing diapers.

"They want to insert a tube through her nostril into her stomach," says my brother. "I told them, 'Nothing doing!'"

My mother is sinking. We are allowing this to happen.

"Her hands were twitching. She was wringing them," says my brother. "And I sat there and held them for an hour until she crossed them and slept."

Two weeks ago I flew to mother.

Only two weeks ago she could still sing.

I'm at her bedside. She's chilled; her teeth chatter.

"Blankets!" she calls. "More blankets!"

At ninety-eight dollars a day, three thousand a month, she should have an extra blanket.

"Make a fire," she tells me.

"There's no fireplace here, Mama."

"I forget," says my mother.

The fire reminds her of a camp song, one she used to sing at Camp *Mechia*.

"An Indian name?" I ask.

"Yiddish," says mother. "Camp Pleasure."

*"Arum dem fayher,
mir zinger lider."*

"What's that?" I interrupt.

"Around the fire
we're singing songs
the night's so beautiful
one never tires."

"ABCA," I say. "That's the rhyme."

"It rhymes better in Yiddish," says Mama. "You know I used to have a good voice."

Today she breathes heavily. Water in her lungs.

The nurse comes to check blood sugar. On top of all her other medical problems, she's newly developed diabetes and has two insulin shots a day.

"How long should we do this to her?" asks my brother when we meet later.

Now my mother turns toward me.

"Campfire days," says Mama drowsily.

*"Arum dem fayer,
mir frelekh tantsn."*

"What did you sing, Mama?"

"I was more thinking than singing," says my mother, "that we, around the fire, were dancing so lively."

I suddenly want to know everything she remembers.

"Take this down," says Mama. "What's my best?"

"Stuffed cabbage," I say.

"Olipses," says Mama. "Sit me up, I can't remember when I lie flat. The thoughts run out of the top of my head."

I crank her up. She remembers stuffed cabbage.

"Cook cabbage, not too soft.
Cool.
1 LB. meat to head of cabbage
Add salt and pepper to taste

also:
sauté 1 large onion
small can mushrooms
raisins."

She pauses, breathing heavily.
An aide pokes her head in.
"*Mamacita*," she says, "how about a little oxygen for dessert?"
With the tube in her nostrils, Mama continues.
"Did I say salt and pepper? Onion? Raisins? Now, mix together.
"Fold mixture inside cabbage
Add one large can tomatoes
Lemon and sugar to taste
Add water to pot to cover mixture
Cook until meat is done by testing with fork."

She leans back. "Did I say lemon? Did I say sugar?"
I nod.
"So, that's *Olipses*."
"Now, meat borscht," I say.
"First, tuna salad," she says, "the kind you and your brother loved
as children."
"I know how to make tuna salad," I say.
"Who's supposed to talk, and who's supposed to listen?" asks my
mother.
"Tuna," she begins,
"Celery.
1 hard-boiled egg
mayonnaise
sweet pickles.

"That's the trick," says mother, "sweet pickles."
"Nobody eats mayonnaise, Mother," I say."Cholesterol."
"So eat it dry," says my mother. "It's your funeral."
I pause a moment.
"How about yogurt instead?" I ask.

"How about mayonnaise half and yogurt half, and it's a deal," says my mother.

"Now the meat borscht," I say.

"I'm tired," says Mama. "While I'm on the IV, I don't like to think of food."

She begins to doze on one elbow.

She's sleeping on my visiting time.

"Tell me more, Mama," I say.

"*Sha, sha,*" says Mama. . . .

She wants to slip away into sleep.

"Any more recipes? Any more songs? Did you sing me lullabies?"

"No," said Mother. "In Russia lullabies were too sad. All about a widow singing her heart out because her little baby will be fated to wander the earth. Who needed it?"

"You mean you didn't sing to us, tuck us in, kiss us nighty night?" I ask, only half in jest.

"I had three hands," says my mother sarcastically, "so I could do everything. Anyway, in those songs, first you tell the baby his misfortune, then you tell him to go to sleep. That's why Jewish children are so serious. . . ."

She lies back. Her hands begin to jerk. Her frown reappears.

"What about love songs, Ma?" I ask.

I am relentless. I want her to stay.

"What's your need?" says Mama. "You suddenly met somebody else? Anyway," she says, "from a Russian Jew, a love song is also a bitter song. The lovers separate, one to marry rich and live in a mansion with crystal chandeliers while the other is left behind, poor and cold, shivering like a leaf in winter."

She stops talking and dozes. She shivers like the leaf in winter. Her hand jerks. The other hand reaches to calm it.

"Sh, sh, *Mamale*," I croon.

I lullaby her until her frown disappears and the pair of hands nestle in each other.

"No invasive measures," my brother is checking with me again by phone. "Right?"

A long hesitation.

"Right," I say.

"That's what we agreed," my brother reminds me.

"Yes," I say softly.

"I've given the Nursing Home the telephone number of the mortuary," says my brother.

I do not comment. He is more efficient than I. And also more caring.

"I'm not the villain in this," he says. "We don't want her to be agitated. Right? And not in pain?"

Does that mean we loosen our grip? We don't wrestle so fiercely with the Angel?

Does that mean we speak of her in the past tense to get used to the sound of it?

Does that mean, if water fills the lungs, we don't increase the dosage of the heart medicine?

If her sugar is high, we stop injections?

This long-distance call is filled with more silence than conversation.

"I read to her tonight," says my brother. "I don't know if she heard, but I read the whole *Jewish News* to her, column by column."

If one is sinking under the water, can one still hear the boat's motor?

"She seemed a little restless," says my brother, "so I sang to her."

"You did?" I'm startled. "What song?"

"A Yiddish song," my brother says.

"But you don't know Yiddish," I say.

"I took lessons," says my brother.

"How come?"

"What you're not given, you take," he says.

"How did it go?" I ask.

"The song?" he laughs.

Unlike me, he can carry a tune. I can carry a load. I can carry my own weight, but not a melody.

I had never heard his singing voice. Even over the phone I'm moved.

"Do you understand the meaning?" I ask.

"Oh, it's a folk song about an old fisherman who went to sea, and he dreamt of fish and love. He ends up getting neither fish nor love."

My mother was right about Yiddish lullabies.

"Come fly by, sometime," I say.

"That could be," he tells me.

Somebody has to sing to me.

Professor Emeritus E.M. Broner's tenth book, Bringing Home the Light: A Jewish Woman's Handbook of Rituals *(Council Oak Books), appeared in 1999. Author of the landmark novel* Weave of Women *(Holt, Rinehart & Winston, 1978), she lives in Manhattan with artist Robert Broner.*

RODGER KAMENETZ

RYE

Inside a caraway seed, half forgotten
a hint of pepper and pepper mint
locked in a small black boat.
In the framework of pores, the breaths
of yeast, the boats slip in
to their holes: The slightly sour
flavor of good Jewish rye—I'm
talking about the white stuff not the black—
also promises sweetness. This contradiction
is how flavor defies logic, how
in the end logic is a silly thing
even though it builds bridges and murders
millions, logic forgets the taste of rye
and wouldn't consider the crust of rye
in all its attributes: firmness, brownness,
circumference and wisdom
for there is wisdom in a crust that holds
the whole within its ellipse,
that restrains the moister whiteness
like the mud shore of a lake in the sun.
Again the seeds are boats. Some genius
thought of them. Probably they have
healing powers, even lodged for days
between the teeth, hitchhikers from an old
sandwich, remembrance of things pastrami.

Rodger Kamenetz is a poet and writer, author of The Jew in the Lotus, Stalking Elijah, Terra Infirma, *and* The Missing Jew: New and Selected Poems. *He lives in New Orleans and is on-line at* http://www.literati.net/Kamenetz.

THE CIRCLE AND THE LINE

According to my son, Disney's *The Lion King* is the greatest film ever made. He saw it three times in the theater, and insisted on playing the sound track every morning on our way to school. All the way to kindergarten, we sang the film's stirring theme song, "The Circle of Life," until one morning I listened to the words.

The Circle of Life may be humanity's most popular idea. Nature is all circles: day and night; the turning of the seasons; the revolutions of planets; birth, growth, maturity, decay, death, and rebirth. The Circle of Life roots human experience in nature and finds the same cyclical pattern in life.

If life is a circle, then death is not an end. Death is not a tragedy. Death is only an invitation to rebirth and renewal. This is the "myth of eternal return"—the phoenix rising from its ashes. No wonder so much of humanity, including Disney, finds comfort in this idea.

According to Joseph Campbell, the circle is the most ubiquitous symbol in world religion. There are Buddhist prayer wheels. The circling of the Kabba in Islam. The circular villages of Native Americans. Christianity, with its faith in death and resurrection, is all circles.

In Judaism, however, you find no circles. Jewish tradition rebelled against circles because it perceived the deadly implications of this belief. Life as a circle is closed, its pattern fixed, and nothing new can enter.

Utter futility!
Only that shall happen, which has happened,
Only that occur, which has occurred.
"There is nothing new under the sun!" says Ecclesiastes.

Can there be a more hopeless idea than the notion that history, like nature, is bound to repeat itself in endless cycles of war, holocaust, plague, and destruction? Can we never learn? Can we never change?

In the Circle of Life, the individual is extinguished. When there's nothing new under the sun, there's nothing new that I, as an individual, can bring to the world. Anything I dream has already been done. Anything I do will only be washed away by time until some fool in the next generation arrives at the same plan and tries again. Ultimately, the Circle of Life is a philosophy of defeat and passivity. If all is fated to repeat, why dream? why try? why bother? Don't worry. Be happy.

Judaism passionately rejected the Circle of Life. It offered a radical new idea: Breishit, *the* Beginning. We are a people obsessed with beginnings. The Torah begins with *Breishit*. Our Days of Awe commence with Rosh Hashanah, the new year. There are actually four New Years every year in the Jewish calendar, according to the Mishnah, including a New Year for Trees. The arrival of a new month, Rosh Hodesh, is celebrated twelve times a year.

To believe in beginnings is to believe that the world can change. That people can change. Destiny is not fixed. Personality is not fixed. You have the freedom to choose to be the person you would be and together, we have the power to create the world as we would want it. No force of human nature, destiny, or heaven can rob us of that freedom, and none can relieve us of its responsibility.

To believe in beginnings is to believe that each human individual is precious, brought into this world to add something totally unprecedented, completely new. Each of us carries one word of God's message. Only with the word of each of us, the contribution of each of us, will the message ever be intelligible, and the world be complete.

....

Ed Feinstein serves as rabbi at Valley Beth Shalom in Encino, California, and as a lecturer in the Ziegler School of Rabbinic Studies at the University of Judaism in Los Angeles. His Torah commentaries appear in the Los Angeles Jewish Journal.

No Time to Rush

"Hurry up, Noam."

"Noam, let's *go*."

"Come *on*, Noam," I implore my four-year-old son. If he does not get into his sneakers more quickly, how will I ever manage to do our errands and make it to the park in time for him to play before lunch?

Brown eyes large and serious, Noam looks up at me. "But I want to feed my horsie," he insists. "Will you help me?"

We have to *go*, I want to say. We'll *never* get to the park. But before I say another word, the story that a friend told me intervenes.

My friend had heard the story from the young widower of her own late friend, Susan.

When Susan was pregnant for the first time, she found out that she had cancer. She miraculously gave birth nonetheless to a healthy baby girl. But as the months passed, she and all those dear to her realized that she was not going to win the battle against cancer. Susan was dying.

During that first year of her baby's life, the only year she would live to experience, Susan had a constant refrain. "*I have no time to rush.*"

No time to rush.

"Here, Noam," I say now with a smile, showing him the toy carrots. "Horses love carrots."

Delighted, Noam holds the carrots out to his toy horse. "Here, horsie," he says. His eyes are even bigger now and his face is radiant.

He is so beautiful, I realize. And how long, after all, will he be asking me to help him feed his imaginary horse?

Ruth H. Sohn

Rabbi Ruth H. Sohn teaches Jewish texts at Milken Community High School and other venues in Los Angeles, where she lives with her husband and three children. She has published biblical commentary, midrash, and poetry. Her commentary on the Book of Ruth appears in Reading Ruth: Contemporary Women Reclaim a Sacred Story *(Ballantine, 1994).*

Jacob Who Loves the Sabbath

God has shown you, O mortal, what is good:
to walk humbly with your God.
　　　—Micah 6:8

For ten years, I served as a congregational rabbi in the suburbs of Orange County, California, delivering many passionate sermons on the holiness of the Sabbath. I spoke of the need to reserve one day each week devoted to contemplation, to community, and to God. Quoting sources ancient and modern, I urged my congregants to abandon the headlong pursuit of elusive chores, of work never completed, and on this one day, to savor, instead, the simple wonder of being. But despite all those years of preaching Shabbat, and even though I myself was Sabbath-observant, I don't think I truly understood my own message or felt the full power of the seventh day until after I left the congregation. It was only after my family moved to the city that my six-year-old son Jacob showed me how to engage in the true soul-rest of the Sabbath.

Jacob gave me the gift of the Sabbath.

Jacob is autistic. His mind perceives the world in ways different from most people; his sense of timing and priorities follows its own inner schedule. The agendas that consume most of us simply don't exist for him. Jacob is indifferent to matters of social status. He loves what he loves, and he loves whom he loves. Jacob is passionate about his family, for example, cuddling in our bed early in the morning, sitting side-by-side as we read together, laughing as we chase one another in the park. And Jacob is passionate about the Torah; transforming a stray branch into a Torah scroll, he cradles it in his arms while he chants the synagogue melodies. Marching his "Torah" around the room, Jacob sings the ancient Psalms of David with same joyous intensity of the ancient singer of Israel.

One of the insights—and challenges—of his autism is that unless Jacob loves it, it doesn't get his attention.

Once we moved to the city and I was freed from my obligation to arrive at services early, to stand on the pulpit, and to lead the congregation in prayer, I looked forward to savoring the early Shabbat morning walk to our new synagogue with my son. On our first Sabbath there, I tried to walk the way most other people walk. I wanted to arrive punctually. Jacob, on the other hand, was already where he wanted to be: enjoying a walk with his Abba. I cajoled, pulled, pushed, yelled, but Jacob would not rush. I told him we were going to miss services, and still he strolled. I insisted that he hurry, and he paused to explore a patch of flowers, or sat himself down in the warm morning sun. I tried grabbing his hand and pulling him by force. I tried walking behind him and pushing with my knees. Nothing worked. By the time we arrived at the synagogue, hopelessly late, my stomach was in knots. I was drenched in sweat, and far too frustrated to pray.

The second week repeated the aggravation of the first. We still reached services late, and I was so annoyed that I couldn't even sit still when we did get to the sanctuary. This last week, I realized that something had to give. Jacob wasn't going to stop being Jacob, which meant that our walk would proceed his way, on his schedule. Resigned to slow frustration, I decided to make the best of it; I would learn to walk the way Jacob walked, but I would take a book.

I chose as companion a medieval mystical text by Rabbi Moshe Cordovero, the Tomer Devorah, "The Palm Tree of Deborah," a meditation on Kabbalah and Ethics.

As Jacob and I and Rabbi Cordovero set out on walk number three, I tried paying no attention to our speed or direction. When I got to the corner, I didn't let myself look at the light—invariably green until right before Jacob caught up. I read.

It's impossible to read quickly while you walk; reading while walking is a form of meditation: savoring individual words, delighting in phrases, I found the words on the page melding into my walk. "Who is like You, God?" the prophet Micah wrote. "There is no moment that people are not nourished and sustained by the Divine power bestowed upon them," responded Rabbi Cordovero. "Thus no persons ever sin against God without God, at that very moment, bestowing abundant vitality upon them. Even though they may use this very vitality to transgress, God is not withholding. Instead the Bountiful One suffers the insult and continues to enable the limbs to move." I could feel the vitality in the words infusing my own, making this very walk a celebration. The sunshine streamed into my soul, God bestowing life and love without conditions or restraint.

As I walked and read, the words of the Tomer Devorah reframed the morning song of a bird into an outpouring of creation's gratitude to God. The egglike flowers of the dogwood trees seemed to gesture the words of the psalmist, "How manifold are your works, O Lord. In wisdom have you made them all." In the towering palm trees we passed, I could feel the call of the prophet Isaiah, "Before you, mount and hill shall shout aloud, and all the trees of the field shall clap their hands."

From time to time, I turned around just to relish my son's meandering. His joy was contagious: the pure delight of a little boy with his Abba and with time. And his joy was pure. My son cannot read, yet his very presence, I could now see, affirmed the words of Kohelet that "there is nothing better than for one to rejoice in what he is doing." Occasionally, I found myself slipping into my old apprehensions, worrying about what part of the service I was missing, or fretting about not proceeding quickly enough. But the allure of my book, the walk, the sun, and my son, restored me. Jacob's spirit had become infectious.

When we finally did arrive at the synagogue, the service was more than halfway over. They were already putting the Torah scroll back into the Ark. Jacob squealed with delight, "The Torah! The Torah!" and ran to the front of the sanctuary. Too excited to stand still, he bounced on his toes next to the person holding the Scroll while the congregation recited the ancient praise: *"Hodo al eretz v'shamayim!* God's glory encompasses heaven and earth!" My spirit soared, for I had just borne witness to that glory in the flowers ablaze in color and light, in the delicate breeze swirling through the leaves. "God exalts and extols the faithful, the people Israel, who are close to God. Hallelujah!"

More than any sermon I've ever heard or given, I owe the fullness of the Shabbat to my son. Jacob taught me through his own example that we can't possibly be late, because, wherever we are, we are already where we are supposed to be. Our minds just have to acknowledge what our heart already knows.

I learned that day that Shabbat is the cultivated art of letting go, letting be, and letting in. In that art, my son Jacob is my teacher, my master, my Rebbe.

My Jacob gave me the gift of Shabbat.

Rabbi Bradley Shavit Artson is the Dean of the Ziegler School of Rabbinic Studies, Bel Air, California, and the author of Dear Rabbi: Jewish Answers to Life's Questions, *forthcoming from Alef Publishing.*

PAYSACH J. KROHN

....

THE ART OF SHARING

Be attentive to the children of the poor,
because from them Torah will flourish.
        —Nedarim 81a

A young man—we'll call him Chezky Silverman—was studying in
a Jerusalem yeshiva and loving every minute of it. His study partner in the afternoon was an ebullient, young, married man, whom
we'll call Yankel Bernstein, and who lived with his wife and five
children in Jerusalem. Yankel's enthusiasm for life and Torah were
contagious.

One Thursday afternoon, Yankel invited Chezky for Shabbat dinner. Chezky delightedly accepted the invitation, for he was looking
forward to meeting Yankel's family. Chezky had been told that the
Bernsteins were poor, but he was not prepared for what he saw in
their apartment. After reciting the blessing over the wine, the *kiddush*, and the blessing over the challah, Yankel cut the loaf into very
thin slices. Could the family be relying on this one challah to last
for all their Shabbat meals? Chezky, who came from a well-to-do
home in Chicago, could not bear the thought.

The meal soon became an anguished ordeal for Chezky, as he
saw the minuscule portions of fish, soup, and chicken that Mrs.
Bernstein served the children. Chezky's own portion was larger
than anyone else's, and he felt guilty, for he understood that he was
being given more at the expense of the Bernstein children.
Although the discussion of Torah around the table and the Shabbat
songs, the *zemirot*, were all lively, Chezky vowed he would never go
there again for a meal. It just wasn't fair to Yankel's family.

A few weeks later, Yankel invited Chezky for a Shabbat meal again, but Chezky said he already had other plans. Again and again, Yankel invited his younger study partner, and each time Chezky had another excuse for not coming. Finally, Yankel understood that Chezky's excuses were just that: excuses.

One afternoon Yankel confronted Chezky directly. "I've invited you over and over again since that Friday night months ago, and you always refuse me. Did something happen? did we not treat you right? was our standard of *kashrut* not up to yours? did any of my children say something that upset you?"

Chezky was surprised at how sensitive Yankel was to his refusals. He couldn't hide the truth any longer. "I'll tell you the truth, Reb Yankel," he confessed. "I had had no idea how you and your family lived. That Friday night, I realized that there wasn't much food to go around the table, and I couldn't bear eating at the expense of your children." Chezky had to hold back his urge to cry.

Yankel put his hands on Chezky's shoulders. "You really are considerate," he said, "but let me explain. I think you'll understand.

"My wife and I come from poor families. When we were married, we decided from the start, that if we were to be blessed with children, no matter how poor we were, we would invite guests for Shabbat dinner, so that our children would learn the value and beauty of *hachnasat orchim*, hospitality to guests.

"We want our children to know that sharing with others is a way of expressing our bounty of blessings from *Ribbono shel Olam*, the Creator."

Chezky understood, but still couldn't allow himself to eat at Reb Yankel's home again. Maybe someday, but not yet.

On the morning of the holiday of Lag B'Omer, Chezky got up in a festive mood and decided to surprise Yankel's children by bringing them a treat. He bought ice cream sandwiches and brought them to Yankel's apartment.

"Look what I brought you in honor of the holiday!" he announced to the children when he arrived.

The children thanked him dutifully, took the ice cream sandwiches, and scampered out of the apartment.

Chezky was taken aback. The Bernstein children could not have been accustomed to having such a treat. Why had they just muttered a few words and run off?

Just a few minutes later, Chezky heard a rumbling up the steps. Before he could turn around, fifteen neighborhood children were clustered around the table in the Bernstein dining room. They were excitedly waiting for the two oldest Bernstein children to come into the room.

In a moment, the two Bernstein boys came to the table, with ice cream sandwiches and knives in their hands. With meticulous care, they sliced the ice cream sandwiches into small portions and handed a section to each of the eager children. Then, in unison, all the children dramatically licked the vanilla ice cream frozen between the chocolate top-and-bottom crackers, smiling and joking as together they devoured their special Lag B'Omer treat.

Reb Yankel stood at the dining room entrance, beaming. His eyes met Chezky's. There was no need for words. What the spontaneous generosity of his study partner's children taught Chezky that day spoke volumes enough.

Adapted from Paysach J. Krohn's collection Echoes of the Maggid: Heartwarming Stories and Parables of Wisdom and Inspiration (Mesorah Publications, 1999). *Rabbi Krohn is a fifth-generation mohel (ritual circumsiser) and the author of five collections of inspirational stories.*

THE CAROB TREE

Throughout his life, a pious man named Honi was troubled by a line in Psalm 126: "When the Lord brought us back to Zion, we were like dreamers." The exile, after all, had lasted seventy years—how was it possible, he asked himself, for a person to hold on to a dream for seventy years?

One day, as Honi was walking down the road, he came upon a man planting a carob tree.

"How long does it take the tree to bear fruit?" he asked.

"Seventy years," the man replied.

Honi was taken aback. "Are you so sure you'll still be alive in seventy years?" he asked incredulously.

The man responded, "I found carob trees heavy with fruit when I came into the world. I plant these for my children, just as my ancestors planted those for me."

Adapted from the Talmud (Ta'anit 23a)

ARYEH COHEN

☉n Fathers and Daughters

As my daughter was forcing her way out of the birth canal; as my partner was undergoing that world of pain and sensation generated by the miraculous architecture of the female body that is beyond my ken; as a clump of matted hair gave way to the radiantly beautiful face I would come to know as Shachar; as I stood watching in awe and reverence, a verse from the Bible forced its way into my consciousness: *vaarubot ha-shamayim niftachu* / "and the curtains of the heavens were opened" (Gen. 7:11). All the pathways from heaven to earth opened. The move from womb to birthing room was the cosmic journey from the celestial place of divine knowing to the finite place of forgetting. At that moment I felt that Shachar opened the curtain just a bit, and I was almost able to see. It was a moment of purity and holiness.

It was the moment that obliterated any possibility for me to understand how a woman is considered impure after childbirth.

The Talmud in *Kiddushin* 30a relates that one morning, as Rabbi Joshua ben Levi was rushing through the streets, disheveled and with child in tow, he met Rabbi Hisda. Rabbi Hisda inquired as to his unseemly hurry. Rabbi Joshua replied, "Is it a matter of little consequence to you that the Torah sets the verse, '*And you shall make them known to your children*' next to the verse, '*the day that you stood before me at Horeb [Sinai]*'" (Deut. 4: 9, 10)? Rabbi Hisda understood that Rabbi Joshua was equating teaching Torah to his child with being present at the Revelation on Sinai. Rabbi Hisda took the words to heart. From that day forward, the Talmud continues, Rabbi Hisda would not taste a morsel of food until he had gone over the previous day's Torah with his child and added something new.

Making breakfast for Shachar in the morning, watching her take in the world, I wonder what it means to teach a Torah that is like being present at Sinai. We sing *"Torah, Torah, Torah / Torah tzivah lanu Moshe /* Torah, Torah, Torah, Moses commanded us Torah," and I wonder whether I am sinking into the banal. Yet, the Rambam in his Laws of Teaching Torah says, "From when is the father obligated to teach his son Torah? From when he starts to talk, he teaches him Torah *tzivah lanu Moshe."* So perhaps this is just the way to start. Perhaps teaching Torah that is regarded as if the teacher were standing at Sinai is not dependent on any specific Torah I might have to teach (an enormous relief). Perhaps it is the interaction itself which is reminiscent of the relationship of God to Israel—as God saw the Israelites wallowing in the blood of their birth and raised them to be present at Sinai. Raised them by *being* present at Sinai (Ezek.16: 6–8; *Mekhilta of Rabbi Ishmael,* "Bo," *Parshah* 5).

But I am brought up short again by the line that immediately precedes the story of Rabbi Hisda and Rabbi Joshua. It is the line that comments on the biblical verse, "And you shall teach them to your sons." The line adds, *"Your sons and not your daughters."*

There is a moment in the life of words and texts that can be located only in hindsight, from a distance. That is the moment when midrash cries out. The moment when the *pshat* (contextual meaning) is mortally wounded and the text bleeds its midrash. It is the moment when the life of a word is radically reconfigured by the life of the community. The writing of the midrash is almost an afterthought. By the time the midrash is known and accepted, the crisis has passed.

In the second century, when Rabbi Eliezer quoted the prophet Jeremiah, *"God will roar from on high, and from God's holy place will give voice, God will surely roar,"* Rabbi Eliezer interpreted Jeremiah's words to mean that there were three watches in the night, corresponding to the three roarings, and that God roared at every watch (*Berachot 3a*). In the next century, in Babylonia, Rabbi Yitzhak bar Shmuel understood the roaring as signifying a cry of mourning. In this reading, God wails three times a night, "Woe to me for I have destroyed my house and burnt my sanctuary and exiled my children unto the nations!" (When the pain of this midrashic bleeding became too awful to endure, some pious copyists changed the text to read, "*Woe is to my children, for because of their sins* I have destroyed my house and burnt my sanctuary and exiled them unto the nations.")

I believe we are standing at, or near, a moment when midrash breaks through the text, though we will not know for a time. When I study the text of *Kiddushin* 30a with a group of men and women, we encounter the midrash about "sons and not daughters" as if we are passing a withered tree in a lush forest. The engagement of the class with the rest of the *sugya* / Talmudic unit is animated, productive—learning that generates insight. This midrash, on the other hand, seems a pallid attempt to account for a redundant phrase ("to your sons")—an attempt that does not impart the possibilities that midrash usually does. We continue to learn the Gemara, but this midrash seems to stand naked—uncovering, in its wake, the verse it was meant to clothe.

It will be Shachar and her friends, reading this text, will see under the torn skin of the text and, covered in its blood, will birth the words that will already have been there always.

The Talmud wrestles with the following question: When there are enough resources to support only one's own study or the study of one's son, which takes precedence (*Kiddushin* 29a)? The Sages of the Mishnaic period, the *Tannaim*, are divided. One says that the father's own commanded obligation to study takes precedence. Another adds the caveat that, if the son is quick-witted and sharp and retains his learning, his study takes precedence over his father's. The following story is told as illustration:

Yaakov sent his son Aha to study at the academy of Abbaye. When he returned home, Yaakov discovered that Aha had not lived up to his expectations. The Torah he had studied was not readily at hand, the teachings were not sharp, the understanding not focused. Yaakov immediately commanded his son to remain at home while he himself went off to study.

Meanwhile, at the academy of Abbaye, all was not well. A demon had occupied the study hall and prevented anyone from entering. So ferocious was the demon that even during the day, when demons usually don't cause harm, and even when students approached in pairs, which usually is an adequate defense against demons, this demon would strike them.

When Abbaye heard that Yaakov was on his way to the academy, he ordered his community to refuse lodging to the approaching sage. Abbaye reasoned that, without a place to stay, Yaakov would spend the night in the study hall and a miracle would occur because of his merit as a sage, and the demon would be defeated.

Yaakov came and found all doors locked to him. As Abbaye had predicted, he went up to the study hall and bedded down. The demon appeared to him as a *Tanin*, seven-headed monster. Now it was up to Yaakov to reclaim the rabbinic territory from the invading *Tanin* of the surrounding culture. Each time Yaakov bowed, one of the monster's heads fell off. Finally, by morning, the sacred precinct of rabbinic lineage was safe.

The story told by the sages reveals how serious an issue they perceived the conflict over resources to be. Going to the heart of the rabbinic enterprise—studying and teaching Torah—and able to be resolved only by deciding whether the father or the son is the better student of Torah, the conflict has the potential to be one of epic proportions. What is at stake in the conflict over resources? As the story suggests, the answer is "everything." For Yaakov recognizes the demon in the study hall as the same *Tanin* whose defeat by God enabled Creation, a defeat celebrated by the Psalmist (*"You smashed the heads of the Taninim on the water"*).

Yaakov understands that the inability to reproduce Sages threatens to undo Creation itself, for this is the tenuous covenant that God struck with Torah and the world.

When learning this passage, I glimpse the life-and-death reality of the obligation of teaching one's children Torah. It is not merely for a trivial sense of Jewish continuity, nor is it part of a handing over of heritage—*it is the world itself which is at stake.* A world that will be maintained only by those who learn and retain their learning and whose learning establishes worlds. The covenant that God struck with Torah and the world—if My children accept Torah at Sinai, then fine; if not, then I will undo creation itself—is at stake with every child who walks into the study hall.

At two weeks I carry Shachar as she cries inconsolably. She does not do this often. Usually she is a very contented baby. As I rock her in my arms I hope that I learn this lesson: I don't always have an answer, a solution. Crying is sometimes what has to happen. I pray that I will always be able to hold her with this same care, love, and equanimity as she cries.

Many nights I rock Shachar to sleep, singing the verses that also welcomed her into the world in her birthing room: *In the name of the God of Israel, to my right is Michael, to my left is Gabriel, in front is Uriel, and behind me is Rafael. Above my head is the Shekhinah of God. Hear o Israel, God, our God, God is One. The Angel who has redeemed me from all evil—may he bless the children and call upon them my name and the name of my fathers Abraham and Isaac and may they multiply amongst the land.* It is a moment that is good and sweet.

Ve-shinantam, and you shall repeat them to your children (Deut. 6:7).

This phrase is prominent both ideologically and liturgically in Talmudic ritual, as it is in our ritual today. Twice a day, marking the boundaries of wakefulness, we repeat this central tenet of rabbinic Judaism: Teach your children Torah.

The Talmud, however, reads this phrase as "And the words of Torah shall always be sharpened in your mouth—*shenunim*. So that if a person should ask you something, do not stammer and tell him, but tell him immediately" (*Kiddushim* 30a–b). Continuing this serious wordplay, the Talmud links phrase to phrase, performing this sharpness with the following stammering tour de force:

For it says, "Say unto wisdom: 'Thou art my sister, etc.' (Proverbs 7:4). *And it says, "Bind them upon thy fingers, write them upon the table of thy heart."* (Proverbs 7:3)

And it says, "As arrows in the hand of a mighty man, so are the children of one's youth." (Psalms 127:4)

And it says, "Sharp (shenunim) arrows of the mighty" (Psalms 120:4) And it says, "Thine arrows are sharp (shenunim) — the peoples fall under thee." (Psalms 45:6)

And it says, "Happy is the man that hath his quiver full of them; they shall not be put to shame, when they speak with their enemies in the gate." (Psalms 127:5)

By citing the sister-lover for whom Solomon so famously lusted, and by whom he was pursued, Proverbs evokes the erotics of study and teaching. The Psalmist then introduces the sharpness that wounds, the sage as hero and gladiator, and finally as victor. At the end of this breathless charge, one question is left unanswered — or perhaps its answer is frightening, disturbing enough to have to be spelled out.

The Talmud asks, "What does 'their enemies in the gate' mean?" When did enemies enter into this most central, most intimate moment of *veshinantam*, of teaching and learning, which started between a father and child, a teacher and student?

Said Rabbi Hiyya bar Abba, Even the father and his son, the Rabbi and his student, who labor in Torah in one gate become enemies to one another. But they do not leave there until they become lovers to one another. For it says, 'et vahev be-sufah [Vaheb in Suphah]' (Num. 21:14). Do not read 'be-sufah' [in Suphah] but 'be-sofah' [in the end].

The teaching relationship is not neutral. It is the "war of Torah" at whose core is not only the future of the world, but the souls of the warriors. The promise is that they will leave the battlefield as lovers. The Talmud performs this transformation with an unintelligible phrase *(et vahev be-sufah)* in a list of battles in Numbers. Cutting into it, eliding the second letter *(tav)* of the first word, then reading the first two words as one, the phrase bleeds love, ohev be-sofah: *"at its end, love."* At the end of the battle of Torah, an end which may be as yet unintelligible to the combatants, is love.

In the end I am left with this. Must all labor go through pain and blood to love? Where is the guarantee that in the end there is love?

The midrash says that the Torah that the Holy One of Blessing gave to Israel is written in black fire on a parchment of white fire. I look at Shachar as she revels in this stage of constant radical amazement, as she begins to articulate the world in a language we can understand, and I wonder: Can we see the black fire on the white fire without being consumed?

....

Aryeh Cohen, Chair of the Jewish Studies Department and Assistant Professor of Rabbinic Literature at the University of Judaism, is the author of Rereading Talmud: Gender, Law and the Poetics of Sugyot. *Shachar Ayala Cohen Hodos is now twenty-six months old and will not take responsibility for the opinions of her Abba. The essay first appeared in* Kerem: Creative Explorations in Judaism *(6: 57–59, 1999).*

SALLY WEBER

Raindrops

On one of those wonderful rainy days when you sit inside sipping soup, listening to the water drip onto the leaves outside your window, my four-and-a-half-year-old daughter and I sat at our kitchen table, looking out at our large expanse of yard. Gavi was intently drawing. She pulled gray crayons for the sky, green and brown for the trees, pinks and purples for the flowers.

Suddenly she became quite pensive. She sat straight up and stared out the window with her enormous blue eyes.

"You know, Mommy," she murmered, "I sometimes wonder if somewhere in the world there's another little girl, sitting at a table just like this one, staring out the window at the rain in a yard just like this one, wondering if somewhere in the world there's another little girl who looks just like her, sitting at a table and staring out the window at the rain in a yard just like hers, wondering if somewhere in the world there's another little girl who looks just like her, sitting at a table and staring out the window at the rain in a yard just like hers."

Then she turned to me and in a dreamy voice added, "Mommy, I think that's what God is all about."

Sally Weber is a licensed clinical social worker in Los Angeles and Director of Jewish Community Programs for Jewish Family Service. She teaches at Hebrew Union College–Jewish Institute of Religion, and has written on the changing Jewish family and Jewish family education.

RICHARD N. LEVY

SHABBAT:
AN ENCOUNTER IN THE
APPLE GROVE

Whether during the days of opposing idolatries among the ancient Canaanites, the warring vulgarities of Rome, or today, amidst the violent ordinariness of fin de siècle North America, we have been rescued from total dependence on the world around us by the gift of Shabbat in Torah.

So vital is the Sabbath, the rabbis teach, that when Adam and Eve ate the fruit on the world's first Friday afternoon, Shabbat herself interceded with God, asking that they not be exiled from the Garden of Eden until the first Shabbat ended. But after Adam and Eve do leave the Garden of Eden, Torah does not speak of Shabbat again until the Israelites are liberated from Egypt. As they entered the wilderness, God sent down manna to sustain them, promising them an extra day's supply on Friday, so they would not have to gather it on Shabbat.

Why did God ask the Israelites to keep Shabbat in the wilderness, three months before the Torah was given? Perhaps because God still remembered Adam and Eve's untrustworthiness, and wanted to test the Israelites before announcing Shabbat at Sinai. Would they obey God this time, and not gather manna on the Seventh Day? God may well have worried: "Look at everything I stopped myself from doing on the Shabbat, from sowing seed to all the other acts that ultimately produced the Creation. How will human beings cease from their labor if when they were in the Garden they couldn't control their appetites enough to leave a piece of fruit on the tree!" Though a few Israelites failed the test, God seemed satisfied that the great majority *were* able to restrain themselves in the wilderness, and so on Sinai, God gave us the Sabbath.

But the nature of Shabbat, as described in *Devarim*, Deuteronomy, had changed. Shabbat was now a commandment—a *lo ta'aseh* commandment, a command *not* to do something, which the rabbis expanded to include all the different kinds of labor from which Jews were to cease on Shabbat: sowing, as God did; harvesting, weaving, cutting, carrying outside, writing, lighting fire, moving too far from one's place—thirty-nine things to refrain from doing. The Talmud calls them the *avot melachah*, literally the "fathers of work," the categories of work fine for ordinary time but forbidden in holy time. In the spaces from which sowing and writing and carrying are absent, there will now dwell the presence, the holiness, of God. This is how the rabbis understand the Shabbat commandment as it appears in Deuteronomy: *Shamor et Yom Ha-Shabbat le-kad'sho*, "Protect the Day of Shabbat, to sense its holiness." On Shabbat, the holiness of God is experienced not only by doing, but by *not* doing—and the more things we don't do, the more Shabbat feels different from ordinary time, and the more holiness fills our lives.

Much later, in the seventeenth century, Jewish mystics created a powerful metaphor for that absence of activity which clears space for the presence of God. Garbed in white, the mystics of Tzfat would walk out into their apple orchards, their *pardesim*, and as they laid down the tools that marked their week, Shabbat herself, they believed, strode toward them, created out of the absence of weekday labor. For the kabbalists, God's holiness manifested itself in the world through seven *sephirot*, seven emanations spun off who knows how long ago from three higher, inaccessible *sephirot*. The seven lower *sephirot* each governed an earthly day, and each represented a different manifestation of God's nature: *chesed*, love; *gevurah*, power or restraint; *tiferet*, compassion; *netzach*, endurance; *hod*, majesty; *yesod*, the sexual center; and finally the seventh *sephira*, the element of God's nature most accessible to us, *Malchut* or *Shekhina*, at one and the same time God's majesty, the feminine side of God, God as manifest in the Community of Israel, as manifest in Shabbat, God as the Divine Presence in the mystics' apple orchard. Each of the six days of Creation has a mate, says the tradition, except Shabbat: and so God gave the Jewish people to Shabbat to be her mate.

Walking through the apple orchards of Tzfat on Friday night, the kabbalists felt themselves to be in the primordial orchards of Eden. For them, it was as though Shabbat had returned to the Garden from her exile, giving humans another chance to show that they could now be relied upon not to eat the fruit: relied upon to refrain from all the acts from which God had asked them to absent themselves.

Where can we find that apple grove today?

In the beautiful, transcendent space created by *not* writing, *not* carrying outside, *not* growing—by not doing the things we are commanded not to do, the *lo ta'aseh*. Turn around the letters of "not" in Hebrew, *lamed aleph*, and there is *aleph lamed*, which spells *El*, one of the names of God. To absent ourselves from work is to discover the fragrant apple grove of the presence of God.

But don't all the *lo ta'aseh* commandments become oppressive, separating us too severely from our neighbors, turning Shabbat into a burden, rather than a gift? Torah answers that question in *Sh'mot*, the book of Exodus. If in Deuteronomy, God tells us to "refrain from the fathers of work," in Exodus, God tells us *Zachor: Zachor* the day of Shabbat, to sense its holiness. What is *Zachor*? Most often, we translate it as "Remember." But after months of not gathering manna one day a week, could the Israelites forget it? No, *Zachor* can't mean "remember"—it means to make present, to bring palpably into our lives, to bring Shabbat down from Sinai into our homes and onto our kitchen table where the candles burn, our dining room table clothed in white, with silver cups gleaming in the light, brimming with kiddush wine, ready to bring Shabbat holiness to our lips. In place of the stern, patriarchal *avot melachah*, the "father-acts of forbidden work," Shabbat as *Zachor* suggests *imot menuchah*, "mother-acts of permitted rest"—our mothers passing their hands over the Friday night candles, bringing forth the challah they had kneaded with their strong, embracing hands—two challot, for the extra portion of manna. But what a difference from the constraints of wilderness! Sweet puffy loaves, their egg whites glistening in the light, the dew covering the manna represented by the challah cover, which those same strong hands had embroidered years before.

In the Shabbat song of the kabbalists, *L'cha Dodi*, "Come, my beloved," we sing: *"Shamor ve-Zachor b'dibur echad"* — *"Shamor* and *Zachor* were said in the same utterance." For the holiness of Shabbat is found in both the evocative *and* the restrictive, the presence *and* the absence, the mothers of rest *and* the fathers of forbidden work. We light two candles on Shabbat precisely to remind us of both *Zachor* and *Shamor*.

To protect Shabbat as a haven from the ordinary week, we need to experience a day without the things we ordinarily are used to and take for granted. *Not* to write down a message means to listen better, to remember more; *not* to drive to the market means to use only what we have in the house, finding satisfaction in whatever we have on hand. Not to putter in the garden means to look at the garden, and enjoy the flowers of Eden; even to refrain from turning on lights can make one so much more aware of the natural changes of color as morning moves to afternoon and twilight. The religious life needs both the absence of ordinary activity and the presence of special celebratory activity; it needs both the femininity of beauty and the masculinity of restraint. The *Siddur* describes Friday night in the feminine and Saturday morning in the masculine — and it describes Shabbat afternoon in both. For the conflict of opposites that mars the weekday dissolves as Shabbat ends, in a messianic harmony.

When God spoke at Sinai, *"Shamor ve-Zachor,* protect *and* make present the Sabbath Day," I believe God knew how much we would need Shabbat to rescue us from an ordinary and chaotic world. If we accept this gift, we too can stroll amid the apple groves; we too can find our lives transformed and Eden regained.

....

Rabbi Richard N. Levy is Director of the School of Rabbinic Studies at the Hebrew Union College–Jewish Institute of Religion in Los Angeles. He is the immediate past president of the Central Conference of American Rabbis, former Executive Director of Los Angeles Hillel Council, and editor of On Wings of Light *(Hillel and K'tav, 2000)*

How a Single Mom Does Shabbat

When I was married, I made an elaborate Friday night meal: fresh challah, chicken or fish, and a special dessert.

I set the table early in the morning and invited guests for the night. Before sitting down to eat, we stood at the table: a hush descended on us, as we lit candles, drank wine and broke bread. How civilized we were.

Now, er, hmm. I am a Single Mom and everything about being a Single Mom is different, including how a Single Mom does Shabbat, the crowning moment of the week.

Of all the family rituals that hold a Single Mom's life together there are two which are most prized: the nightly reading of the bedtime story, and the Sabbath family meal.

Whatever it does for my daughter, the bedtime story keeps me sane each evening, as Samantha and I mark our progress through *In the Night Kitchen* or my old favorite, *All of a Kind Family.*

But Friday night belongs to us in a separate way, a time dedicated not to fantasy stories but to reality, our reality, in our own home.

As a Single Mom, I have been sitting on the freeway for more than an hour by the time I get home from work on Friday evening. I am looking forward to a good meal. Throughout the week, naturally, I eat on the run; the regulation muffin-and-coffee breakfast, dinner from the take-out section at our local market, which I eat with a plastic fork directly from the container held on my lap as I drive home.

But Shabbat is different and it demands something which is eaten off a plate.

Pushing my way through the door, my arms loaded with groceries, I take off my shoes and kick them into the corner, dump the packages onto the kitchen counter, and preheat the toaster oven. I take four fish sticks out of the box in the freezer and dump them on a foil-lined metal toaster tray for broiling. I slice two carrots, toss them in a steamer and set the stove on to "high." So much for Friday dinner for Samantha.

As for me, I throw a baked potato in the microwave. In roughly ten minutes, I'll mash the potato with Parmesan cheese. And steamed broccoli—the plate needs color—and viola! Eat your heart out, Julia Child.

Running to the dining room table, I shove a week's worth of mail to the side. I take the store-bought challah out of the bread box and set it on the silver platter, alongside the candlesticks and a wine cup. Samantha takes out the candles; having forgotten to buy wine, I pour Sundance cranberry drink into the silver goblet, hoping God will forgive me.

"Come on, Sam, let's do Shabbat," I call to my daughter now engaged in her 3,000th viewing of *Jaws*. Getting no response, I go after her and slam the tube off.

"OK, kill the lights," I say. She hits the switch and we're in darkness. For a brief moment, Samantha and I look at each other, in thanksgiving for the week just passed. We say the prayers over the wine and bread and offer a quarter to our charity box for the poor; she eats her fish sticks in the living room watching *Jaws: The Avenger*, a rented videotape. I eat my baked potato in the dining room, setting my plate on a pile of bills.

By 8:30 we are both asleep.

Being a Single Mom has given me a new understanding of human fallibility. I have not yet bought whipped cream in an aerosol can, but I once picked it up longingly before buying the kind you beat from scratch. It's not that my standards are lowering, but here are some words I no longer use: "perfect," "correct," "spotless."

My mother used to tell me that the key to happiness is the ability to "look away," that is, the refusal to take seriously every dust ball under the couch, every dirty nail on a child's hand. Boy was she right: a Single Mom soon learns to love her blinders, she lives with the constant knowledge that the cat needs its shots, the linoleum is peeling, and the checkbook remains unbalanced for the second year in a row, but how much can you do?

Oh well, Single Mom rests on the seventh day from her labors and says not that "This is perfect" but that "This is good enough."

All right, so I'll never get it perfect. Maybe accepting the fact is a relief. All around me, baby boomers with their new families are still aiming for perfection, the best stroller, the best kinder gym, starting their kids reading at six months. They long to create a "spiritually perfect" child, creative, perky, a Harvard MBA or a star in TV commercials, a child who won't rebel.

Once I was like them, somewhat smug, convinced that life is like a vast test kitchen in which the object is to get out all the kinks in the recipe. But I'm learning the hard way: There is no one recipe! There is no single right way! And if there is, *I'm doing the best I can!*

And anyway, gourmet education is bankrupt unless it teaches the basic, eternal values of hard work, kindness toward others, and respect for oneself.

I guess being a Single Mom has only made explicit what I've always guessed: Life's path is often lonely, but there is no alternative.

The children of Israel wandered forty years in the desert, most of it in circles, gaining spiritual fulfillment.

Nothing happens overnight.

The point, if there is one, is to discover, in Leo Baeck's words, the holiness in everything, by which I suppose he meant even a dinner of fish sticks and microwaved potato. In our nightmares, our tragedies, we know God too.

Single Mom gets ripped off by the auto mechanic, sweet-talked by the electrician.

Taking out the garbage, I try to find the holiness here, but it's hard.

In the perfect Shabbat, each person blesses the other: the husband blesses his wife as a "Woman of Valor." The parents praise their children as worthy descendants of Abraham and Sarah.

Shabbat dinner over, Single Mom sits down by Samantha and nibbles on the little girl's carrot.

The killer shark has returned.

"I love you," I say.

The little girl nods.

"I love you, too, Mom."

One holy moment is good enough.

November 1987

Marlene Marks is the author of A Woman's Voice *(On the Way Press, 1998) and the editor of* Nice Jewish Girls Growing Up in America *(Penguin, 1996). A journalist and syndicated columnist, she lives in Malibu, California.*

TOURISTS

They arrange condolence calls when they visit us:
they sit at Yad VaShem, have grave faces at the Western Wall,
and laugh behind heavy drapes in their hotel rooms.
They have their pictures taken with our famous dead
at Rachel's Tomb and Herzl's Tomb and on Ammunition Hill
they weep for our handsome youth
and lust for our tough girls
and hang up their underwear to dry quickly
in cool blue bathrooms.

Once I sat on the steps near the gate of David's Citadel with two heavy baskets next to me. A group of tourists stood around their guide and I became their point of reference. "See that man with the baskets? Just right of his head there's an arch from the Roman era. Just a little right of his head." But he's moving! he's moving! I told myself: Redemption will come only when their guide says: See that arch from the Roman era? It doesn't matter: but right next to it, a little to the left and down a bit, there's a man sitting, who bought fruits and vegetables for his family.

Translated from the Hebrew by Miriyam Glazer

Yehuda Amichai is one of Israel's foremost writers. His poetry has been translated into more than twenty languages. Among his most recent works in translation is Selected Poetry, *translated by Chana Bloch and Stephen Mitchell (University of Berkeley, 1996), and* Open Closed Open, *translated by Chana Bloch and Chana Kronfeld (forthcoming from Harcourt, March 2000).*

Rabbi Shimon Bar Yochai and the Fire

The great sage Rabbi Shimon bar Yochai devoted his entire life to Torah. When the Roman occupiers intensified their persecution of Jewish study and practice in Palestine, he, his student Rabbi Elazar, and his son, took refuge in a cave so that they could pray and study. A carob tree and a spring trickling through the stone walls miraculously supplied them with food and water.

Twelve years passed.

One morning, the prophet Elijah stood at the mouth of the cave. Peering into the darkness, he called, "The Caesar has died! His decrees have been nullified!"

The three men, hearing the news echoing through the cave, ventured into the sunlight. Slowly they made their way back along the stoney paths to the farms and villages of Palestine. Everywhere they looked, life seemed to be going on as usual: The farmers were ploughing, children were gathering eggs, women hanging out laundry, shopkeepers briskly at work selling.

Rabbi Shimon's rage burned within him until he exploded. "How dare you fill up your time with such ordinary tasks!" he berated them. "How dare you neglect even a moment of prayer!"

He blazed with such anger that the farms and villages and towns caught fire, and everything Rabbi Shimon had gazed upon was consumed.

The earth trembled in shock and then grew silent.

From the heavens, a *Bat Kol* / Divine Voice sobbed, "Rabbi Shimon, Rabbi Shimon, have you come out of the cave only to decimate my world? Go back! You don't belong here!"

The voice of Rabbi Elazar cracked through his parched throat. "The wickedness is ours," he whispered.

Rabbi Shimon nodded in shame. "The tradition teaches that the wicked dwell in the hell of Gehennom for twelve months," he said.

And for twelve months, Rabbi Shimon, Rabbi Elazar, and Rabbi Shimon's son did.

PERHAPS

Toward the middle of our heated encounter, he threw his arms around me and protested his love for my Jewish soul, my *yiddishe neshama*. With a firm lock around my shoulders, he insisted that, together with all the Jews of the world, the two of us were together at Sinai even though differences in theology and religious observance divide us today.

I felt caught. To free myself from his grip would seem a rude rejection, but to return his embrace with my own would be false. I felt neither love nor scorn for this intense, bearded rabbi, ten or fifteen years my junior, whom I had never seen before that night's lecture.

"Rabbi," I said, "you may love my Jewish soul, but *mein neshama iz nisht kein rozhenke*—my mind is not a raisin. You show no respect for my Jewish mind, my interpretation of tradition, my commitment to pluralism."

"There is only one tradition," he persisted. "*One* law, *one* way, *one* guide."

We parted company and later that night I sat up wondering what I had expected of this unquestioning man so absolutely certain that only his view of Judaism had divine sanction. Perhaps, I thought, that is the nature of the True Believer: a person who never entertains the smallest possibility of doubt. But if spiritual certainty is what matters, how shall we interpret these three stories?

EFSHAR

The village atheist, the *apikoros*, boasted one day that he would shortly confront the leading Rebbe of the community with incontrovertible proof that God does not exist. The villagers loyal to the Rebbe warned him of the planned onslaught. As sure as the sun stood still at Gibeon, at midday the *apikoros* entered the Rebbe's home filled with anticipatory glee.

The Rebbe welcomed him and the two sat down to eat a hearty lunch. Just as the *apikoros* was about to deliver his carefully prepared speech proving beyond doubt the nonexistence of God, the Rebbe set down his fork, sipped his water, and said "*Efshar.*"

"*Efshar,*" he repeated. "Perhaps."

With this, the *apikoros* burst into tears. He rose from the table, reached out to the Rebbe, and the two embraced.

WITH ALL MY HEART AND SOUL

Once, it was told in the name of Rebbe Menahem Mendel of Kotzk, a troubled young man came to the Rebbe. He confessed that his faith was shattered. He had lost his belief.

The Rebbe listened and responded gently, "Why, my son, can you no longer believe?"

"Because the world seems to have neither rhyme nor reason," the young man cried. "Violence, injustice, and cruelty are rampant. The righteous suffer and the wicked prosper."

"So," said the Rebbe. "Why does that matter to you?"

"What do you mean, why does that matter to me?" the young man retorted. "In such a cruel world, there is no justice, and if there is no justice, I doubt whether there is a God governing the world."

"So," the Rebbe persisted. "What difference does it make to you if there is no God in the world? Why should you care?"

"Rebbe," murmured the young man with growing frustration, "if there is no God in the world my life makes no sense. It has no meaning."

The Rebbe touched the hand of the tormented young man. "Do you care so much about the world? about the existence of God?"

"With all my heart and soul, Rebbe."

"Ah, my son, if you care so much, if it pains you so much, if you doubt so much, you believe."

Harold M. Schulweis

THE TRUE REBBE

It happened once that the disciples of a beloved Rebbe were forced to leave their village for another. So they went to their Rebbe and asked him for advice. When they settled in their new village, how were they to identify another Rebbe as authentic as he?

"When you meet the village Rebbe," he counseled them, "ask him whether strange thoughts ever arose in his prayers. Ask him if he was ever possessed by doubt. If he answers that he never had strange thoughts, that he never suffered doubt, know that he is not a true Rebbe and he should not be followed."

Faith is a peculiar gift, neither the last word, nor the first. Faith is like a window: When we shut it firmly, we keep out the "strange thoughts," but also the fresh air; when we carelessly leave it open, we invite the blustery wind. Allowing our window of faith to be both open and shut is a spiritual task that takes both wisdom and courage.

Harold M. Schulweis is a rabbi at Valley Beth Shalom in Encino, California. He is founder of the Jewish Foundation for the Righteous and author of For Those Who Can't Believe *(HarperCollins, 1994).*

THE CONVERTS

On the holiest day we fast till sundown.
I watch the sun stand still
as the horizon edges towards it. Four hours to go.
The rabbi's mouth opens and closes and opens.
I think: fish
and little steaming potatoes,
parsley clinging to them like an ancient script.

Only the converts, six of them in the corner,
in their prayer shawls and feathery beards,
sing every syllable.
What word
are they savoring now?
If they go on loving that way, we'll be here all night.

Why did they follow us here, did they think
we were happier?
Did someone tell them we knew
the lost words
to open God's mouth?

The converts sway in white silk,
their necks bent forward in yearning
like swans,
and I covet
what they think we've got.

Chana Bloch

SPIRITUAL SECRETS

Three years ago, with only one year of rabbinic school behind me, I spent the summer working as a hospital chaplain in my hometown of Chicago. Most rabbinic students wait until their fourth or fifth year to venture into the world of chaplaincy, but I was determined to get out and do something "rabbinic." So off I went to Northwestern Memorial Hospital for eleven weeks of "Clinical Pastoral Education."

Every morning I met with the patients on my assigned floor, and every afternoon I talked over my experiences with my five fellow-chaplains, all of whom were Christian ministers-to-be. Their accounts of their hospital adventures intrigued me. They would all report on how they had seen patients So-and-So, had talked with them, had listened to them, and, finally, how they had prayed with them.

Prayed with them? I didn't really grasp what they meant. On the one hand, I thought I was pretty open-minded about prayer. I relished my own private prayer time. I recognized the value of praying in English. On the other, I couldn't imagine what they were actually *doing* when they prayed "with" people. Soon, though, I realized that when I walked into patients' rooms and introduced myself as The Chaplain, many of the Christian patients were eagerly expecting me to do just that.

One day, I just bit the bullet. I asked a patient if he wanted to pray. He nodded his head and breathed a great sigh of relief.

"Out loud?" I murmured.

"Yes."

"Would *you* like to speak? . . . or should I?" I asked.

"Oh, you, please," he responded.

So this was it. This was what chaplains were supposed to do. I took a deep breath and opened my mouth, and, with the patient at my side, I talked to God.

It's not as if I had never talked to God before—just never out loud, never in English, and never, certainly, in someone else's presence. From somewhere and somehow, though, the words came to me. We prayed for his return to health. We prayed for us to be able to feel "God's presence." We prayed for strength and courage and the ability to feel the love and support of family and friends.

And then I said, "Amen." And then he said, "Amen."

And what do you know? I had prayed with someone.

He looked relieved. He looked satisfied. He seemed quite a bit more at peace, and so, I imagine, did I.

In the days and weeks that followed, I continued to pray with the Christian patients. The more I did, the more convinced I became of such prayers' tremendous power—to bring comfort, to connect people deeply, to transform a time of pain into a holy experience.

I was inspired enough to raise the subject with the Jews in the hospital. But I never knew quite *how* to ask Jews. For one, many of the Jews regarded the whole position of hospital chaplain as a threatening Christian imposition.

"Would you like to pray?" "Would you like me to say a blessing?" No matter how I phrased it, the offer fell on defensive, distrusting ears.

"I don't do that!" "I'm not religious!" Time after time, I heard those words. The Jewish patients would happily describe their grandchildren's bar mitzvahs, or lament some relative's intermarriage, or comment on how interesting it was that I, a woman, was going to be a rabbi. But *prayer?* As soon as I mentioned it, they shuddered.

And yet, if they would let me stay in the room with them and continue to talk, nine times out of ten they would eventually confess that while they lay in their hospital beds, they too talked to God.

And quickly add: surely I, The Rabbi, would have no interest in such talk. Surely what they were doing was not *Jewish* prayer. After all, their prayers hadn't come out of a synagogue-sanctioned prayer book and they weren't in a language they didn't understand.

Their Jewish selves and their spiritual selves were entirely separate.

In the months and years that followed, I grasped that what was true for the Jewish patients at Northwestern Memorial Hospital in Chicago was also true for many of us Jews. Being Jewish was okay. Being "spiritual" was also okay. But being a spiritual Jew or Jewishly spiritual—that was a contradiction in terms.

The price we pay for that inner split was driven home to me just this last summer, when I took a job at the only halfway house in the country for Jewish ex-cons, drug addicts, alcoholics, gamblers, anorexics, and compulsive overeaters. I was apprehensive when I got to Beit T'shuvah in Los Angeles, for I had no prior experience with addictions, and no idea how a bunch of drug addicts and criminals, men and women from 18 to 65, were going to receive my own twenty-five-year-old female rabbinical student self.

Two months later, I wasn't sure of what the residents of Beit T'shuvah had learned from me. But I knew what I learned from them.

Despite my experience as a chaplain, I saw that most of my life I had regarded my Judaism as a valued life companion, a wonderful set of tools, a nice family to have been born into. But for the men and women of Beit T'shuvah, all of that may or may not have mattered, because for them Judaism is a *lifeline*, perhaps the only lifeline that can take them out of their slavery to an addiction and guide them toward the promised land of life. At Beit T'shuvah, I saw, it's *cool* to strive to cultivate one's Jewish soul—one's spiritual self. Not just cool—encouraged, prized, talked about eagerly and openly. Torah is *necessary*. Judaism is *necessary*. God is *necessary*. For them, not to have a relationship with the divine is to suffer spiritual death—if not physical death as well.

But are the addicts, the alcoholics, the gamblers, the only ones among us who are broken? Are they the only ones who are incomplete? For the residents of Beit T'shuvah, the void within was palpable, desperate—and perhaps it is *because* they feel that void so acutely that, when they are ready to try, their souls are able to inhale deeper breaths of God. But how many of us also feel an inner emptiness we scramble in so many ways to fill? What if we, too, allowed ourselves to admit that *something is missing in our lives*, if we, too, allowed ourselves to share our pain with God, if we, too, allowed ourselves to breathe in the presence of God, and fill the voids within *us?*

And what if, like the Christian patients at the hospital, and like the recovering souls at Beit T'shuvah, we shared those spiritual wrestlings with one another? For even if we are observant Jews, even if in our own individual ways we murmur our personal prayers to God, many of us do so in secrecy—under our tallises, beneath our covered eyes, behind our prayer books. Even if we stand in the midst of the congregation, we are alone. But what if we Jews began to emerge from our spiritual closets? What if we were to discover that others among us talk to God before going to sleep? And others among us write to God in journals?

Were we ever to utter the words and the home-made prayers aloud to one another that we murmur so silently to God in our journals and beds, we might experience the unbelievable comfort of sharing our spiritual secrets with other Jews.

Sarah Graff is pursuing rabbinic ordination at the Jewish Theological Seminary. She holds a degree in psychology and Jewish Studies from Washington University in St. Louis. She is also the author of an interactive children's prayer book, published by Camp Ramah Darom.

THE POWER OF PRAYER

A voyaging ship was wrecked during a storm at sea. Only two of the men on it were able to swim to a small desert island.

Stranded on the island, the two realized that their only recourse was to pray to God. To find out whose prayer was more powerful, they agreed to divide the territory between them in half and stay on opposite sides of the island.

The first prayer was for food. The next morning, discovering a lush fruit-bearing tree on his side of the island, the first man ate to his heart's content. On the other side, he noticed, the land stayed barren.

A week later, the first man grew lonely. He decided to pray for a wife. The very next day another ship foundered on the island's rocky shore, and the only survivor was a woman. She swam to the first man's side of the land. No one and nothing came to the other's side.

Delighted with his success, the first man then prayed for a house, for clothes, for more food. Like magic, all he had prayed for arrived the next day. But still the second man had nothing.

Finally, the first man realized that he should pray for a new ship so that he and his wife could leave the island. In the morning, a handsome clipper appeared docked right on his beach.

So the first man boarded the ship with his wife and got ready to set sail, leaving the other man behind. Having had none of his prayers answered, hadn't the other man proved unworthy of God's blessing?

But no sooner had he raised the anchor then a voice boomed out of the heavens. "Why are you leaving your companion on the island?"

"He doesn't deserve to come!" the first man responded. "His prayers went unanswered! The blessings bestowed on me are clearly mine alone!"

"How mistaken you are!" retorted the Voice. "Your companion had only one prayer, which I answered. If not for that, you would have received nothing at all."

The first man lowered his voice. "What did he pray for that I should owe him anything?"

"He prayed that all of *your* prayers be answered."

For all we know, the blessings that come to us are not the fruits of our prayers alone, but those of another, praying for us.

....

This story was transmitted to me by Barry Leff from "somewhere on the Internet." Barry Leff, a former high-tech CEO, cab driver, restaurant manager, bouncer, pilot, and flight instructor, is now a rabbinical student. He lives in Los Angeles with his wife and four children.

STACIE CHAIKEN

A Valley Girl Midrash

Rabbi So and So tells the story of how when Rivka the chicken seller was beset with a fever that had her shivering in her bed for thirteen days, the spirit of her father came to her and said, "Get up, my Rivka, and go to the fields. A small, white flower blooms on the western edge. Pick seven petals and seven leaves, no more, no less. Come back and make yourself a tea."

"But Father," cried Rivka, "I am sick! I haven't left my bed for thirteen days!"

"Go my Rivka, I promise you. All will be well."

And so she went and she made the tea and she drank it, and all was well.

When I was three years old, we moved from the East Coast, where I was born, to Covina, California. We bought a little tract house on East Hurst Street, a cul-de-sac, at the end of which had once been orange groves, long ago razed for a housing development. But the developers ran out of money, and the land reverted to desert, which is what most of Los Angeles County used to be, before irrigation.

Neither of my parents had ever lived in a real house before — only apartments. Now, though, was going to be different; now was going to be new. Daddy had got himself a ton of education, a good job: We crossed the mountains, the prairies, the plains — just as my parents' parents and grandparents had crossed the Atlantic to America! Land of Opportunity! So we bought this house with a yard and some trees (Peach tree! Banana tree! Birds of

Paradise!) on a manicured block, at the end of which was, basically, this huge, chaotic desert (Tumbleweed! Snakes! Gilla monsters!)

It was a Catholic neighborhood. We were the only Jews. My folks are both from Brooklyn: Brooklyn, New York, Land of Much Better Bagels and Lox Than You Can Get at the Corned Beef King on Citrus Avenue In Covina. Nothing in Covina—or anywhere else, for that matter—was as good as it was in New York. I learned early on: This may be the Sunshine State, but New York (where all the good Jewish food is) was my hometown.

I would disappear for whole days in that wilderness at the end of the block, building forts, chasing lizards, with my Catholic heathen friends. Their mothers would come after them at lunchtime, but never mine. My mom might stand at the end of the street and yell for me, but no way she was going to set foot beyond the suburban sidewalk. The desert dust might sully her yellow suede shoes. Which matched her yellow knit dress with the blue stripes, the yellow fishnet stockings, the yellow leather clutch, and the yellow straw hat. This is what she wore when she came to pick me up from school. There was no place to hide.

When I was six years old, my mother's beloved father, my Grandpa Clarence, died of a heart attack in New York City. I vividly imagined him clutching his chest, collapsing on the sidewalk in the shade of the Empire State Building. My mom and her sister, Auntie Tiby, flew east for the funeral. When they got back to Covina, my mother sat me on her lap and assured me that when her father died, the trunk of his car, a light metallic blue Chevrolet Impala sedan (!!!), was packed with all his worldly possessions—all his clothes, his books (Grandpa Clarence was a scholar), and so many beautiful presents for all of us kids. He loved us so much, he was on his way to live with us in California. And this was incredibly sad, because he died and I never knew him. I insisted on sitting shiva, learned the Mourner's Kaddish by heart, dovened with the *altakakers* at the synagogue. I lit *yahrzeit* candles for him, year after year. Clarence was my first great friend among the dead.

Age twelve, puberty. I start asking questions: How come I can't shave my legs like everyone else? How come we're so Jewish, we have bacon for breakfast? How come Grandma Ann and Auntie Tiby were living in Los Angeles when Grandpa Clarence died, and he, Grandma's husband, was living in New York? And whatever happened to all my presents from the trunk of his car? That's what I want to know.

Auntie Tiby comes clean. She's a scientist, devoted to truth—like my dad, like me. Turns out, she tells me, three years before he died, the saintly Grandpa Clarence suddenly ran off to Mexico, divorced my Grandma Ann, remarried, and had had no contact with my mother or the rest of the family since that time. His trunk was not packed; there were no presents. God only knows if he even owned an Impala—or what color it was.

Still, my mother clung to the story of her father's trunk being packed and him being on his way. As an adult, after I moved to New York City, she would visit me and tell that same bogus story. Again, and again, in dimming twilight hotel rooms, over half-empty bottles of cheap white wine and pretzels.

And then there was another story about how several years ago she was dying of cancer, and the doctors said there was nothing they could do: They were letting her go. And that's when, she says, her dead father Clarence came to her in the hospital, and he said "It isn't time."

So my mother told my father, "Clarence says it isn't time," and my father went to get the doctors and told them, "It isn't time," and therefore they should go ahead and try this dangerous cutting-edge experimental therapy they'd been hedging on. Because it wasn't time.

And the therapy worked, and my mother got better. And so, my mother says, her father saved her life.

Could be.

Rabbis tell lots of stories just like my mother's. They assure us that they are true. But does that mean that they're based on fact?

As for Clarence, there is ample evidence to suggest that my mother's story about her father's trunk being packed and his being on his way to live with us in California is not based in fact. But who is to say that it is not true? Maybe it was his aching heart that was packed, and not his steel blue trunk? Who is to say? And who is to say that when my mother was dying, the spirit of her dead father did not, in truth, come to save her life?

Not me. Not a word. I never said a word. Even all those years I thought my mother was, well, not in touch. She was just deeper in touch. With her own story, her own ravenous longing. Her truth.

....

Stacie Chaiken is an actress and writer living in Los Angeles. She is the author of A Wish Book *and* Looking for Louie, *a solo play she also performs, about a Russian Jewish American (sometimes) Redhead who goes off in search of the mysterious great-grandfather about whom nobody would ever speak.*

Pastrami on Rye

Two hours after breakfast at the Stage Deli in New York City
I sit with my mother and my aunt ready to order lunch.
My aunt has been fighting stage 4 cancer for three years.
"What are you having?" she asks us.
I choose tuna. Then turkey.
"Meatloaf," says my mother. "Or matzo ball soup."
My aunt nods her head. Smiles. A piled-high
pastrami sandwich walks by. We change our minds.

My aunt has tried to eat organic since the diagnosis.
The doctors say the cleaner diet (no poisonous pesticides, no
body-altering hormones) has sustained her life.
But my aunt won't go all the way, won't deprive herself
of food. "It's part of life," she says,
"the best part." When the weary waitress arrives at our table
we order the pastrami. My aunt compromises—a salad, though
not organic. The waitress scribbles in code and leaves.
"Hey, miss!" she calls. "I'll have
pastrami on rye, too."

And suddenly I see my aunt on Yom Kippur,
prayer book menu in hand. She pounds
her fist to the chest harness she has worn for three years
to keep her bones from snapping. Fist to chest
against her own long history.
The sandwich approaches. She knows
pound she can never measure up *pound* alone

she is not enough. She prays for solace
pound and is delivered a piece of heaven sandwiched
between two slices of rye. *Pound, pound, pound.* She bites.
Smiles. Now she turns to us to ask,
"What time should we eat dinner?"

*Ronda Spinak, a Stanford graduate, is a writer living in Los
Angeles. Her plays include* Killing Mother *and* Oscar Wilde's Wife.
She has recently completed My Mother's Kitchen, *a collection of
poems.*

Why Jews May Be Famous for Answering a Question with a Question

Once upon a time, a man who had been secular all his life woke up in the middle of the night with a longing to learn Talmud. The very next morning, he went to the Rabbi of his local synagogue.

"Rabbi," he said to the surprised Rabbi, "I would like to learn Talmud."

"I am delighted!" the Rabbi responded. Wary that the man's enthusiasm might wane as quickly as it had awoken, he added, "So we begin now. Here's a question for you: If two men climb up a chimney, and one comes out dirty and one comes out clean, which one washes himself?"

The man was surprised by the naïveté of the question. "The dirty one," he answered immediately, thinking to himself, "*This is Talmud?*"

But the Rabbi shook his head. "No, not the dirty one. They look at each other and the dirty man thinks he is clean, and the clean man thinks he is dirty. So the clean man washes himself.

"Now, another question. If two men climb up a chimney, and one comes out dirty and one comes out clean, which one washes himself?"

The man smiled and said, "You just told me, Rabbi. The man who is clean washes himself because he thinks he is dirty."

But the Rabbi again shook his head. "No," he said. "If they each look at themselves, the clean man knows he doesn't have to wash himself, so the dirty man washes.

"Now, a final question," he continued. "If two men climb up a chimney, and one comes out dirty and one comes out clean, which one washes himself?"

Ah, thought the man to himself, *I begin to understand.* "Well, Rabbi, it could be the clean man and it could be the dirty man. It depends on your point of view."

But the Rabbi, shaking his head, responded, "No. If two men climb up a chimney, how could one man remain clean? They both are dirty, and they both wash themselves."

The man was entirely baffled. "Rabbi, you asked me the same question THREE TIMES! And every time you gave me a different answer. I came to you in all earnestness—and what you reward me with is some kind of a joke."

The Rabbi shook his head one last time. "No. This is not some kind of a joke. This is Talmud."

....

This traditional tale was transmitted to me both by writer David Brandes and by Rabbi Elliot Dorff, each of whom got it from . . . who got it from . . .

JONATHAN OMER-MAN

Fish:
a Story

Once a year, at the beginning of March, Rabbi Joel Kentucky went to his tailor to be measured for a new suit. The garment was to be ready before the festival of Passover, when Rabbi Joel presided over the opening of the new session of the rabbinic court. He didn't really need a new suit, but he had to be seen in one. It was a professional obligation. After wearing his new suit just once, he would give it away. When he had first arrived in our city, Rabbi Joel had tried a number of different tailors, but for several years now he had been going to the same person, Chaim Bergenzon. Many religious Jews went to Chaim for their suits, for he was a righteous man, and was known to be scrupulous concerning the biblical prohibition of fabrics that use both wool and linen. Rabbi Joel enjoyed his yearly visits to Chaim; he liked talking with him, for the tailor was an astute observer of people and was a student of both the revealed and the concealed, and he liked watching the man as he worked, throwing and folding and cutting and sewing the cloths.

But Chaim Bergenzon was also known for his sharp tongue, and on that particular morning Rabbi Joel felt a little apprehensive about his appointment later in the day. He knew that Chaim was likely to make some comment about his weight, and he was disinclined to discuss the matter with him. For the truth of the matter was that Rabbi Joel was enormously overweight, and he possessed a ravenous appetite. But serious as such matters might be, they should be discussed between a man and his physician, or perhaps between a man and his Creator, but certainly not between a learned rabbi and his tailor. It was not that Rabbi Joel was a pompous cleric who did not speak with ordinary folk but rather that he was a very private person. He had not set himself apart from the people; rather, he had dedicated his life to the quest for holiness. If in our days the word *saintly* can still be used to describe the living, probably no person in our city was more deserving of the appellation than he. He was devout in his prayers, courteous in his demeanor, pious in his outlook, and meticulous in the fulfillment of his duties. He studied the holiest books of our most secret tradition and strove to live in purity. Notwithstanding, he ate seven pounds of fish on each and every day, except, of course, on fast days.

In fact, the confrontation with the tailor was easier than he had feared. Looking at Rabbi Joel standing in his underwear in the measuring room, Chaim said: "Rabbi, you are not living your life properly. Overweight is overweight, fat is fat, obese is obese, but you are more than all of them. Something is wrong, and you should go to a doctor."

Rabbi Joel sighed, "I know, but will you make me my suit?"

"I shall make you your suit, I shall make you a suit," said Chaim, "and it will be ready before the opening session of the rabbinic court. But tell me, will you go to a doctor?"

"Yes," said Rabbi Joel, "you are right. I shall go."

They fixed an appointment for the first fitting, and Rabbi Joel went home.

Rabbi Joel lived by himself in a large apartment that comprised the entire top floor of the rabbinic college. There he slept and he worked and ate and offered counsel; there too he prayed, at dawn and at dusk, alone in his private synagogue. Only on the Sabbath did he go downstairs to worship with the faculty and students of the college. Rabbi Joel had lived alone since he had arrived in our city, shortly after the death of his wife. His children and grandchildren visited him occasionally, but though they felt welcome, they also knew that their presence was not required; he was self-sufficient. At sixty-five years old, Rabbi Joel was following a path that needed no personal intimacy. Furthermore, during their previous visit, his youngest granddaughter had cried in the night and said that she could not sleep because of the stink of fish.

As he came home that day, Rabbi Joel thought to himself that it was true, and that not only his apartment, but the whole college was beginning to stink of fish. Perhaps his eating habits would bring him into open conflict with his colleagues, some of whom were already uncomfortable with his path, and could even bring the entire institution into disrepute. The tailor's words, "Rabbi, you are not living your life properly," echoed in his mind. Chaim was right, and he would go to the doctor. "But tonight," he thought, "I am going to eat my meal of seven species from the great sea."

He placed the seven fishes on the grill tray, one-pound slabs of cod, haddock, hake, halibut, mackerel, sea perch, and sole. He laid them from right to left, in alphabetical order, and garnished them with a sauce of butter, garlic, and salt. He did not make the same arrangement of the fishes under the grill every night, though for several years he had been using these seven species. He was still looking for an order that would be correct both objectively and subjectively. Sometimes he arranged the fishes alphabetically according to their Hebrew names, or by the distance of their habitats from Jerusalem, the depths at which they lived in the ocean, and even their colors. And although the order he had adopted that evening was still tentative, he placed the fishes in the tray with precision and certainty.

Rabbi Joel set the table and then he recited his afternoon prayers. His timing was always right, and as he read the final verses the familiar smell of roasted fish reached his nostrils. He scrubbed his hands thoroughly from the elbows down with soap and a hard brush; only then did he take a laver to perform the ritual ablution of his fingers. He sat down at his table and spent a few minutes contemplating the slightly charred and smoking offering before him. At such moments, he often wondered why fishes had never been accepted as sacrifices at the altar in the Temple in Jerusalem. Among all the creatures of the animal world, none seemed to know their place better than fishes. They swam, they spawned, they ate, they grew, and they died, all in the darkness of the abyss; in a mysterious fashion, they seemed to be able to live in harmony and abundance while being cut off by the waters from the blessing of light. They fulfilled their function in the world of silence.

Rabbi Joel made the appropriate benedictions and slowly ate his meal. He noted the taste, the texture, and the smell of each fish, both singly and in combination. His meal was made up of seven courses, each of which had seven parts. The first course was of cod: first he ate a portion of cod; then a portion of cod with a small piece of haddock; then a portion of cod with a small piece of hake; then a portion of cod with a small piece of halibut, and so on, until he had eaten a portion of cod with a small piece of each of the other six species. The second course was of haddock: first he ate a portion of haddock; then a portion of haddock with a small piece of cod; then a portion of haddock with a small piece of hake, and so on, until he had eaten a portion of haddock with a small piece of each of the other six species. By the time he had completed the seventh course, that of sole, and had eaten the final portion of sole, that with a small piece of sea perch, two hours and forty-five minutes had elapsed. Throughout the meal he strove to remember the source and the destination of each morsel, what he was raising, and what he was separating. Rabbi Joel ate as befits a holy man—but he ate too much.

He did not eat so much out of greed. Indeed, he was hardly aware of his body during these meals. True, he enjoyed the pleasures of tasting and chewing and swallowing, but not the sensation of gorging himself. Rather than heavier, he felt lighter when he was done. For Rabbi Joel, eating was a rite of sanctification, not relief for his physical appetites.

The following day Rabbi Joel kept his promise to the tailor and made an appointment to see a physician that very afternoon. He was referred to the metabolic disorders clinic, where he was weighed, measured, and questioned about his diet. A medical student measured the circumference of his ankles, calves, thighs, hips, waist, chest, wrists, forearms, biceps, neck, and head, writing his findings down on a multicolored chart; the young man looked puzzled, sent

Rabbi Joel to be weighed again, and made his calculations several times over. A male orderly asked him for a urine specimen, and a nurse took his pulse, his blood pressure, and his temperature. He sensed that he was the center of a flurry of interest, that people were looking at him furtively, and then hurrying on to their tasks. And then, and this is scandalously common in the medical clinics of our city, he was abandoned, just left to sit alone in a corridor for a whole hour while important people in white coats rushed past.

Eventually he was summoned to the doctor's office and was surprised to see not one physician but a medical tribunal of three. Were they dressed in black instead of white, he thought, they could pass as a rabbinic court. So this is what the other side looks like.

The elderly doctor who sat between the other two opened the proceedings without introducing himself. His voice was deep and gentle, but also controlled. "Rabbi Kentucky," he said, "it is our policy in this clinic to be open and candid with our patients. And that is the way we would like to be with you." He paused, and Rabbi Joel, knowing that the doctor was waiting for him to acknowledge the authority of medical science that was invested in his person and in this tribunal, nodded seriously. The doctor continued: "Rabbi Kentucky, not only are you seriously overweight, but you are also much too heavy."

Now Rabbi Joel was known for his sharp talmudic mind; he could discriminate between the finest points of law, between the subtlest nuances of language, but the doctor's distinction was beyond him.

"What's the difference?" he asked.

"It's quite simple," explained the doctor. "There are two separate problems. The first is that for a man with your body structure and height, your weight should be between 150 and 165 pounds, and it is 245. Now this is quite serious, and we will tell you later about the strain that this places on your cardiovascular system. The second problem is that when we look at your bulk, that is, at how big your body actually is, we find that your weight should be only 220 pounds. So not only is there too much of you, but what there is is too heavy. Let me explain the second problem differently. Human beings normally have the specific gravity of sea water; that is, they can float on the water. You would sink. Even with a life belt, you would sink."

The two younger doctors nodded in concurrence.

"I should go on a diet?" asked Rabbi Joel.

"We would like to admit you to our advanced metabolic studies research department. Today. Immediately. If you have to make arrangements at home or at work, you can go and come back this evening. But you must eat nothing and drink only water."

Rabbi Joel thought of the forty-two pounds of fish in his freezer, sighed and said, "I can do what has to be done with a couple of telephone calls. Let's start."

And so he became a hospital patient. He was stripped of his clothes, given nicely ironed hospital robes, and settled in a room in the top-floor of the building. The whole east side of the city was visible from his window, and in the distance he could see the high flat roof of the rabbinic college. A student from the college brought over his prayer-books, his phylacteries, and prayer shawl. Visitors were not encouraged.

Day after day they starved him and they tested him. His intake was limited to water and pills. He rode stationary bicycles; was connected to a variety of electronic devices; gave blood, sputum, and urine every few hours; was x-rayed from every conceivable angle; and was weighed every twelve hours.

On the fifth day, Anna, the young nurse who weighed him, told him that he had already lost twenty-four pounds.

On the sixth day he made a telephone call to Chaim Bergenzon, the tailor, saying that he was already so much thinner that Chaim should stop working on the suit. No, he preferred no visitors. He would call about a new measuring when he got out of the hospital.

On the seventh day he was once again summoned to the medical tribunal. "We are doing very well with the overweight problem, Rabbi Kentucky," said the elderly doctor whose name he did not know. "You have lost thirty-three pounds. At this rate, within a week we will have conquered the medical problem of your excessive weight. We can start giving you some solid foods. However, Rabbi Kentucky, I must admit that with your second problem, the fact that what is left of you is too heavy, too dense, we have drawn a blank. It's a medical mystery. To tell the truth, your condition has worsened. You are now even denser than you were before."

"So what do we do?" asked the rabbi.

The younger doctor at the left answered. "We have one clue. We don't know what it means, but we have to follow it up. In the x-rays that we took there were shadows over various parts of your body; they were especially heavy in the thoracic region. We immediately suspected some metallic deposits, like lead, but none of the tests revealed any traces of unusual ions in your body fluids. So we are left with no explanation. What we would like to do is to move in a radically new direction."

Rabbi Joel sighed. "Tell me what is necessary," he said.

The young doctor continued. "We want to take a biopsy of your pericardial tissue, where there are particularly heavy x-ray shadows, and to submit the material to micro-chemical analysis. We need your consent to do this."

"You want to stick a needle into my heart, and you want me to agree?" asked Rabbi Joel. "Fine. I trust you. I consent."

The biopsy was taken within an hour, and despite the local anesthesia, it was quite painful. After he was returned to his room, he slept for a couple of hours. He was awakened by Anna, the young nurse, who gave him his first solid food in a week: grapefruit and low-fat cottage cheese.

The tests continued over the next few days, and though nobody told him about the progress of the investigation, he sensed a growing excitement. The medical student who took the blood samples said nothing, but seemed to look at him in wonderment. More x-rays were taken with sophisticated equipment that, he was told, gave a three-dimensional picture. The young doctor who had sat to the left of the elderly doctor came twice, once to ask him about the exact quantities of the fish that he had eaten every evening, and once to inquire where he had purchased them.

On the seventh day after the biopsy he was summoned once again to the medical tribunal. There were nine doctors. A hanging court, he thought. They were very courteous to him, treating him like an

honored guest, not like an overweight patient in the metabolic disorders clinic. They asked him to be seated, and he noticed that the
hard-backed chair he had previously been offered had been
replaced by a leather conference chair.

The elderly doctor opened the proceedings.

"Rabbi Kentucky," he said, "last week we told you that your loss of
weight was encouraging, but that we were concerned about what
appeared to be metallic deposits throughout your body, especially in
the thoracic region. Well, I am pleased to tell you that by now the
first, that of your overall bulk and weight, is effectively under control. And about the second, we have a diagnosis. That is what we
would like to talk to you about."

Second-from-the-right, one of the new physicians, continued:
"Pleased to meet you Rabbi Kentucky. My name is Eugene
Newman, from the National Micro-Isotope Laboratory in
Washington, D.C. I was called in when all the standard chemical
tests of your biopsy failed to reveal anything. Your physicians here
concluded that the deposits in your body must be of an inert metal.
I tested the material and found that it was gold."

"Gold?" asked Rabbi Joel.

"Yes," continued the young doctor who had sat on the left at the
first tribunal, who had come to ask him about the fish that he ate,
and now was sitting on the far right. "Gold. A lot of it. The first
question we had to ask ourselves was where so much gold had
come from. I had a look at the fish. According to what you told us,
you have been eating about 22 kilograms of fish a week for a
period of seven years. That means that you have eaten just over
56 metric tons. Now I have consulted with my colleague here,"
and he nodded to the man to the left, who nodded in return,
"Dr. Flannigan, a noted ichthyologist, and he has informed me
that such fishes may contain up to one hundredth of one percent
of pure unassociated gold. One hundredth of one percent of
56 metric tons is 5.6 kilograms. And in your body we have found
5.45 kilograms of unassociated gold."

The elderly doctor in the middle continued: "Rabbi Kentucky,
5.45 kilograms is about 12 pounds. At yesterday's spot price in

Geneva, $419 per ounce, you are worth $80,448. About four-fifths of the gold is in the area of your heart, so that alone is worth about $65,000."

"Please stop for a moment," Rabbi Joel interrupted him. He closed his eyes for a few moments, trying to understand. He opened his eyes. "Please continue," he said.

The elderly doctor continued. "The physiological process by which pure unassociated gold has been deposited in your body is a mystery. It is within the cells, in an atomic state, in a colloidal suspension . . ."

"Excuse me, doctor," Rabbi Joel interrupted him, "but I have a question for Dr. Newman. Did you find only gold? Or were there other metals too? I mean, was there silver? Is the gold alloyed with silver?"

Dr. Newman looked surprised. "Yes, there is silver too, but it's present in much smaller quantities. About five percent by weight."

The elderly doctor continued: "The silver is not worth more than $500. But Rabbi Kentucky, what I wanted to tell you is that your medical condition is apparently not threatening to your health. The gold is inert, and there is no danger of poisoning. It is not affecting any of your essential functions. Your heart, liver, kidneys, are all fine. But the gold should not be there, and it is important that we discover how and why you have absorbed it."

Rabbi Joel interrupted the doctor once again, this time with considerable agitation. "Stop, please stop," he almost shouted. "Gentlemen, learned doctors, please stop. I must leave you now. I can hear no more. I truly appreciate everything you have done, all your work and all your care, but now I must leave. I am truly grateful, but I can stay here no longer. As you have just said, my condition is not serious, and with your permission, I shall go home now."

For a few minutes the learned doctors lost their professional reserve. There was uproar, as all spoke and shouted together. Then each in turn urged him to remain in the hospital and to let them continue their research. "Our findings will advance all of medical science." "We have called a news conference tomorrow to announce a major discovery. We'll have to cancel it." "You may possess the secret of human beings' making gold." "Your name will go down in history. We were going to call the condition Cardius Midasius. We'll change the name to Cardius Kentuckyius." "Please, Rabbi Kentucky, please."

But Rabbi Joel would listen to none of their please. He thanked them courteously for all their help and insisted that he be permitted to leave the hospital immediately. "Gentlemen, I must go," he said. "I have just ten days to get a new garment made and to prepare for the opening of a new session of the rabbinic court. To say nothing of preparing for Passover. I have been away from my duties for too long. Thank you, learned doctors." And with this, he got up, went to his room, got dressed (and discovered that his clothes were much too big) and went to the office to sign himself out.

He did not go straight home, for he needed time to think, to understand. "We have found gold in your heart," the physicians had said. "You are not living your life properly," the tailor had told him. He walked through the city, from park to park, occasionally resting for a while on a bench, and then moving on. He knew that he was being drawn in a specific direction, but he could not go straight there. Nevertheless, after a couple of hours, he reached the basement workshop of Chaim Bergenzon.

"Rabbi Chaim," asked Rabbi Joel, "you knew about all this, didn't you?"

"Yes," answered the tailor softly, "but please don't call me rabbi."

"You knew about it all. About the fish, about my meals, about the gold."

Chaim shrugged and offered his guest a chair.

"Chaim," said the rabbi, "for seven years I've been working on my eating. For seven years I've tried to make each meal into a perfect act of worship. It was the most important thing in my life, to do just that one thing perfectly. And what happens? I got almost a hundred pounds overweight, and a crazy doctor tells me I've got $65,000 worth of gold in my heart."

"You made some mistakes, Rabbi Joel," said the tailor. "You made some mistakes."

The two men sat together in silence.

After a few minutes Rabbi Joel said, "What should I do? Chaim, can you tell me what I should do?"

"What do people do when they make mistakes? They try to correct them."

"Can you help me, Chaim?" asked the rabbi.

"Rabbi Joel, you've chosen the loneliest of paths. It might take you to great heights, but it is the loneliest of paths. You know that. You know that I can't tell you what to do. I can tell you when I think you're making a mistake, and I can wish you well-being. But that's all." The tailor paused for a moment, and then continued: "But you know, there is one thing I can do for you. I can make you some new clothes. Rear garments, not a suit to hide in at a ceremony once a year. Real clothes that you can wear every day of the week."

There was nothing more to be said. They made an appointment for a new measuring, and Rabbi Joel left. He took a bus home. To enter his apartment he took the service elevator at the back of the building. He did not want to be seen, and he told no one downstairs of his return. For many years Rabbi Joel had not been as agitated and distracted as he was that afternoon. He moved restlessly around the apartment, never staying in one place for more than a few minutes. He went to the freezer and looked at this fish piled up on the shelves, and was unmoved, or rather, he was moved in a direction he did not understand and could scarcely feel. He went to the closet and was baffled to see that indeed he possessed no clothes. From his library he took down some sacred books, reread the well-marked passages on fish, and looked up what he could on gold and silver, but he knew that he would not find the answers there.

Just before sunset he went into his private synagogue and began to recite the afternoon and evening prayers, but he could not concentrate. The familiar benedictions and exaltations moved through his throat and his mouth, but they did not flow from his soul. Strange thoughts danced in and out of his mind; they appeared so rapidly and were so bizarre that he could not follow them, could not see where they came from or where they were going. At such times, he knew, prayers were unacceptable, and though they should not be abandoned or abridged, they should be concluded as quickly as possible.

That night Rabbi Joel prepared a final festive meal. He placed the seven fishes on the grill tray, one-pound slabs of cod, haddock, hake, halibut, mackerel, sea perch, and sole. He said them from right to left, in alphabetical order, and he garnished them with a sauce of butter, garlic, and salt. As the fish cooked, he just sat and watched. He did not get up to set the table and did not prepare himself for dinner. He did not get up to perform the ritual ablution of his hands. This night he would not participate in the meal. When the familiar odor reached his nostrils, he did not remove the fishes from the grill, but left them until they were charred, until they were totally consumed. The acrid, bitter smell brought a welling up of tears to his eyes, and still he sat. Only when a pillar of black smoke billowed from the oven and began to fill the room did he get up. He opened all the windows of his house to let the smoke blow away, out into the city, high into the clouds, and beyond.

....

Jonathan Omer-Man is president of Metivta: a center for contemplative Judaism. He is a rabbi who has spent many years teaching Jewish meditation and spirituality, and in personal spiritual counseling, and wishes he had more time to be a writer.

SONGS OF INNOCENCE
AND EXPERIENCE

There is a fountain in a sacred deed.
—Abraham Joshua Heschel

A fine freedom a thrill
flows along our vertebrae
when we demonstrate
for peace for civil rights to save
the bluegreen planet, when we perform
acts of chesed some
call it holy spirit
some call it shekhina

Imagine a fountain
a clear stream rippling downhill
as winter ice creaks breaks up

imagine stiff curled leaves
branches frozen in snowdrifts
imagine sap rising in maples, wet granite
boulders starting to dry
a bear meandering wide awake
somewhere in the woods
squirrels leap chitter
over miles of beech pine birch
imagine the scent

Alicia Ostriker

Some call it the endocrine system,
rapture in the adrenals is the
reward of goodness, like sex
or eating it
pours all the way through
the libido the ego the superego—
we feel alive then

So do the thief, the liar,
the killer, the conqueror,
the enraged
envious as a black hole—

tiger, lamb, tiger
raccoon—

we are that mixed animal
you are that mixed god

Alicia Ostriker's most recent books of poetry are The Mother–
Child Papers *(Beacon Press, 1990),* Green Age *(University of
Pittsburgh, 1989), and* The Imaginary Lover *(University of
Pittsburgh, 1989). She published* Unwritten Volume: Re-thinking
the Bible *(Basic Blackwell) in 1993.*

Rabbi Nachman
and I

I was never much of a follower. During the sixties many of my friends and associates sought out masters to guide their lives. Some were gurus, some psychologists, some teachers. I couldn't see the appeal of giving up my independence to someone else. Anyway, I didn't like to take orders. Just as I steered clear of fraternities, I avoided cults of every kind. It's true I did have an excessive attachment to Bob Dylan, but his motto was "Don't follow leaders."

Somewhere along the way I read Martin Buber's *Tales of the Hasidim* and, astonished by its power and profundity, I went on to read his retellings of the Baal Shem Tov and Rabbi Nachman of Bratslav. Something of Buber's romance of Hasidism clung to me. Though the figure of the Baal Shem Tov was compelling but distant, that of his great grandson Rabbi Nachman, a Tzaddik who was also a storyteller, had a strangely powerful appeal.

The more I read about him, the more my fascination grew. I began to read the translations of his tales as they had been recorded by his loyal scribe, Rabbi Nathan of Nemirov. In the last four years of his life, Nachman would sometimes tell a new story to his Hasidim on a Friday night, after the Sabbath meal, knowing that his scribe could not write it down until the Sabbath ended. The whole Shabbat the Hasidim would tell the story over and over again among themselves, in order to lose as little of it as possible. They were compelled to contemplate the story and seek to discover its many meanings.

Nachman's followers believed that their Rabbi had concealed his most secret teachings in the garb of the tales. Though "The Lost

Princess," for example, appears to be a simple fairy tale about a princess who disappears after her father says, "Go to the Devil!," followed by the epic quest of the king's minister to find her, for the Bratslavers the tale has a mystical meaning. For them, the king is God; and the princess, the Divine Presence—the *Shekhinah*—the Bride of God and Sabbath Queen; and the loyal minister, the Messiah. For the Jewish mystical tradition teaches that since the destruction of the Temple in Jerusalem, the *Shekhinah* has been in exile from God, and will remain in exile until the Temple is rebuilt in the messianic era. For Rabbi Nathan, the minister is every Jew: We must all search for the lost princess and bring her back to God.

For many years I had considered myself a Jungian, but after reading Rabbi Nachman, I began to feel like a secret Bratslaver as well.

One incident in particular confirmed that allegiance. I was living alone in Israel. It was Rabbi Nachman's *yahrzeit*, when the Bratslavers read from his stories all night. I really wanted to join them, but none of my friends were able to come with me, and I was reluctant to go alone. I was home by myself, when all of a sudden there was a knock at the door.

"Who's there?" I called out. A man answered, saying it was a yeshiva student collecting old clothes. Collecting old clothes on that night of all nights! Terrified of who might really be there, I refused to open the door. Whoever it was eventually left. In confusion I picked up a book of Rabbi Nachman's stories and opened it at random. I read one word: "music." Instantly, a story came to me, complete from beginning to end. I wrote it down quickly. It described Nachman being carried off by a fiery chariot, like Elijah, and taken on a heavenly journey that includes a vision of "The Celestial Orchestra," which became the story's title.

Though I had turned away the visitor, I had received the gift he was bearing: the story.

"The Celestial Orchestra" inspired me to imagine an epic tale about Rabbi Nachman, in which he would be the hero, much as the heroes in his own tales. For the entire three months in which I wrote "The Captive Soul of the Messiah," I felt that Rabbi Nachman himself was my muse. The story tells of Rabbi Nachman's epic quest, accompanied by his Hasid, Shimon, to free the Messiah's soul, which is being held captive by the Prince of Darkness.

By the time I finished it, I was so enthralled with the figures of Rabbi Nachman and his closest disciples that other tales followed with great momentum. In the end I discovered that, inspired by his powerful spirit and vision of the world, drawing on his teachings, dreams, and fragments of tales as well as my own imagination, I had written a fictional biography of Nachman.

By the time *The Captive Soul of the Messiah: New Tales About Reb Nachman*, appeared, I sensed Nachman's presence on a daily basis, his warnings, his blessings, his affirmations. He had become a sacred companion guiding me toward the spiritual realm. The Bratslaver Hasidim believe that the powerful spirit of Nachman has been wandering ever since his death. That spirit was as vivid to me as that of my father.

Two fathers
guide me
wherever I go.

One
will never abandon me.
The other
has escaped
from the tomb
to be here.

Even now
they are waiting for me
to follow.

And I did follow: I began to write versions of Nachman's own tales, and included them in all my collections of Jewish folktales. These include some of his best-known stories, such as "The Lost Princess," and some of the most obscure, such as "A Garment for the Moon."

Sometimes it seems that Rabbi Nachman looks for me when I forget to look for him. One of his tales I hadn't paid much attention to was "The Merchant and the Pauper"—that is, until I was approached a few years ago to assist in the writing of a folk opera based on that tale.

Rabbi Nachman entered my dreams. In one dream I learned that he was still alive and living in London. In another, I asked him for advice, and he told me to go ahead and tell a story—and since that dream I have slowly undertaken to become a storyteller. I dreamed that after the death of Nachman's father, his mother disguised herself as her husband and pretended to be him. Though she came close to being caught, Nachman's followers saved her and guarded her secret. In a fourth dream I told a version of Nachman's tale, "The Prince Who Was Made of Precious Gems," combining it somehow with "Rapunzel." The story ends with a precious jewel emerging from Rapunzel's little toe.

When Nachman died, say the Bratslavers, his spirit chose to remain in this world rather than accept his heavenly reward. Once Nachman told his followers that if they would visit his grave in Uman and recite ten particular psalms in the correct order, he would pluck their souls from Gehenna and raise them to Paradise. To this day the Bratslavers make a pilgrimage to the Rabbi's grave on Rosh Hashanah, and they regard at least one such visit in their lives as an obligation.

Nachman is also said to have told his Hasidim that there was no need for them to appoint a successor after his death, for he would always be their Rabbi. Though this instruction went contrary to the ironclad Hasidic tradition of appointing a new Rabbi upon the leader's death, the Bratslavers obeyed Nachman, and to this day regard him as their master. Rather than wither away without a living Rabbi, the Bratslavers have flourished by letting Nachman's teachings and tales guide them.

Rabbi Nachman's wandering spirit can have a powerful healing presence. When Rabbi Yisrael Ber Odesser was a young man, he mistakenly ate on the fast day of the Seventeenth of Tammuz and as a result fell into such a deep depression that he even contemplated suicide. Searching for a reason to live, he used a traditional Jewish method of divination, *Sheilat Sefer*, opening a book at random, as Nachman himself sometimes did. Rabbi Yisrael closed his eyes and took down a book from the shelf. When he opened his eyes, he realized that the book was one of Rabbi Nachman's. Inside it, he discovered a letter tucked among its pages:

"It was very hard for me to descend to you. My precious student, be strong and courageous. My fire will burn until the Messiah will come. As a sign that this letter is true, on the Seventeenth of Tammuz they will say that you are not fasting."

The letter was signed "Na-Nach-Nachma-Nachman of Uman." After this story became known, signs appeared all over Israel with this coded name.

This letter transformed Rabbi Yisrael's life, and he always maintained that Rabbi Nachman had sent it to him from heaven.

Later, when the revered Rabbi Abraham Isaac Kook, Israel's first Ashkenazi chief rabbi, came to the Holy Land in 1904, it was widely known that some kind of change came over him. Even his handwriting changed. "I am the soul of Reb Nachman," he was heard to say. Some followers believe that the soul of Nachman, who also loved the land of Israel passionately, had been reincarnated in Rav Kook—or perhaps that when Rav Kook set foot on the Holy Land, the soul of Nachman fused with his own.

Much more recently: when Israeli writer Yehuda Yaari, who was close friends with the philosopher Martin Buber, writer S. Y. Agnon, and scholar Gershom Scholem, was working on a Hebrew edition of Nachman's tales, he wrote entirely from memory, he told me. Or rather from dictation: he swore he heard Nachman's voice reciting the tales, and, like Nathan of Nemirov before him, he wrote down what he heard. Perhaps that is why Yaari's retellings of Nachman's tales are among the most inspired.

Of all the tales of the wandering spirit of Rabbi Nachman, the most astounding is the saga related to me by Matti Megged of Nachman's intricately carved chair. Trying to escape from the Nazis, the Bratslav Hasidim had been forced to cut Nachman's chair, their most precious memento, into pieces. Vowing to meet again in Jerusalem, each one was entrusted with a single piece.

Every Bratslav Hasid who carried a piece of Rabbi Nachman's chair arrived safely in Jerusalem.

Today, perfectly restored, it stands in the Bratslav synagogue in Mea She'arim.

I will never forget the first time I saw the chair in that synagogue, right next to the Ark. Its very existence spoke volumes; it was like being in Rabbi Nachman's presence. Afterward, descending the stairs of the synagogue, I felt embraced by a vibrant wind, as if it had rushed up the stairs to greet me.

I knew it was Rabbi Nachman.

Professor of English at University of Missouri–St. Louis, Howard Schwartz has published poetry, fiction, children's books, and a four-volume set of Jewish folktales. Next Year in Jerusalem: 3000 Years of Jewish Stories *won the National Jewish Book Award in 1996.* Reimagining the Bible: The Storytelling of the Rabbis *was recently published by Oxford University Press.*

GOD PROVIDES

Rabbi Herschfelder sat at his kitchen table, carefully crafting his Shabbat sermon, as he always did on Thursday afternoons. It was raining hard outside—so hard, in fact, that flood warnings had been blaring from the radio and television all day. The rabbi's roof had begun to leak, so he placed some pots around the room to catch the water, while his mind focused all of its energy on trying to find a more vivid metaphor, a more powerful sentence for his sermon. The phone rang, interrupting him.

"Rabbi, are you all right?" came the worried voice of his faithful congregant Rebecca Bender. "Is your house flooding? I'm right outside in my car, please please join us—we're driving to higher ground."

The rabbi smiled to himself. "There's no need to worry about me, Rebecca. I'm not in danger. I'm working on my Shabbat sermon and if I need God's help, I know He'll provide it," he calmly responded.

"But Rabbi, what will you—!"

"Don't worry, don't worry, dear. Just take care your children's photos shouldn't get wet!"

Rabbi Herschfelder hung up the phone, and sat down again at his now soggy desk. The water had begun to slosh around his ankles, so Rabbi Herschfelder murmured a prayer to himself, put his legs up as he wrote, and continued to craft his sermon.

A rapid knocking on the door interrupted him. Arnie Winnblatt was standing at the entrance, a frantic expression on his face, an oar in his hand. "Rabbi, Rabbi!" he cried, "the street has turned into a river and the water is rising. I've got a canoe outside and you've got to come with us."

The rabbi grinned confidently. "Thank you for thinking of me, Arnie. But, really, there's no need to rescue me. God will take care of me, you just worry about taking care of your family!"

"But Rabbi—!"

"Really."

Arnie shrugged reluctantly and went on his way, shaking his head.

But the rain poured down worse than ever, the house filled with water, and Rabbi Herschfelder finally found himself having to climb onto the roof. His head tilted toward the sky as sheets of water came flooding down from heaven. The house swayed beneath him, just as Ida Levy swooped down in an emergency medical helicopter.

"Rabbi!" she hollered over the deafening rain and swirling propeller. "Come aboard fast! We don't have much time!"

But what need did Rabbi Herschfelder have of a helicopter? "Thank you, thank you, lovely Ida," yelled the rabbi over the roar of the water, "but I have loved God all my life with all my heart and with all my might, and I know that He won't fail me now! God will come to my rescue!"

"Rabbi—but Rabbi!"

"No, no, go and rescue those who need it! Try Aaron Alexander's house; he hasn't been to services in months! He needs saving!"

Ida realized her helicopter rescue of the Rabbi was to no avail, and sadly motioned the pilot to fly on.

Still it rained. The Rabbi clung to his antenna and prayed ever more fervently as the water rose and rose, until it reached his waist. His chest. His neck. The crown of his head. And the Rabbi drowned.

Moments later Rabbi Herschfelder found himself inside the pearly gates. There was a disappointed scowl on his wet face.

"Rabbi Herschfelder, my faithful servant! What in my name are *you* doing here?" a puzzled God asked the frowning Rabbi.

"Funny you should ask," mumbled the Rabbi. "Fool that I am, I put my trust in you to save me from the flood."

"Fool indeed!" said God. "Who do you think sent the car, the boat, and the helicopter?"

The Restoration

In the beginning when God created the Universe, He decided to have some fun and create a world made entirely of paint. So He put on an enormous smock, mixed some colors with celestial light, and lifted his heavenly paintbrush.

God went to work. He worked long and hard and when He was finished He was ecstatic. This was no ordinary painting. It was huge and beautiful beyond belief. Then a thought occurred to God that perhaps he should sign His work. After considering it, God decided that this was too self-important, so He kissed the painting instead.

Now God's kiss had a very strange effect on the painted planet. It suddenly sprang to life. The painted trees began to sway in the wind. The painted birds took flight in the blue, blue sky. The painted people began to wake up and move about in this, the most lovely of all created worlds.

It was more than God had hoped for. A living painting. God's kiss had given the planet a life of its own.

Now God's presence on this planet was mysterious and not that easy to detect. Still, the painted beings were aware of their Creator because rays of light from his celestial paintbrush shone through on every surface.

The painted world gave God much joy and solace. Whenever he was wearied by more troublesome planets elsewhere in the Universe, he would turn and gaze at his colorful creation. It was a peaceful place where the people treated the animals and the trees with real kindness and respect.

The living painting multiplied and grew. Centuries passed. Societies came and went, but the delicate light from God's paintbrush was still visible. Even in the noisy cities that had begun to appear.

Then a strange thing happened. A young man who lived on the painted planet looked around and began to wonder, "Why is it only God who gets to paint?" he thought. "Why shouldn't I be able to paint as well?"

The young man thought about this and thought about it until it became an obsession. "Who does God think He is?" he asked his friends. "I can paint, too, and I'm going to do it!"

The young man's friends tried to stop him but he pushed them aside. He raced to the hardware store, bought a can of spray paint, and took it into the street. With his friends looking on, the young man began to spray his "creation" on the walls, the sidewalks, even on the trees.

Everyone waited for lightning to strike but strangely, nothing happened. "You see?" said the young man triumphantly. "The Creator doesn't care if I paint! Who knows? Maybe The Creator is just a myth . . . Maybe he really doesn't exist at all." The young man finished his painting with a flourish and then boldly signed his name to it.

The sight of his name glowing on the wall gave the young man a tremendous sense of pleasure. He ran back to the hardware store and bought more spray cans. The young man no longer wanted to paint pictures. He just desired to spray his name, again and again, on every surface he could get his hands on.

Now, huge and curious crowds surrounded the young man as he worked. At first the people scoffed, but soon others became possessed by the desire to paint, and little by little, inch by inch, the celestial light from God's paintbrush began to be covered over.

God was heartbroken as he watched his creation turn on him, but what could He do? God's kiss had given these creatures freewill and freewill included the possibility of going wrong. God's sorrow grew as thousands and then millions of people began to deface the glory of his original painting.

Years passed. The wondrous world that had once given The Creator so much joy was now his heaviest burden. Generation after generation of painters had sprayed, scribbled, and chalked over every surface of the planet. It was no longer beautiful. Now, it was a dark and gloomy place inhabited only by depressed artists.

Into this grim world, a young girl was born. Now this little girl was different. All of her friends wanted to grow up to be artists, but she wasn't so sure. The young girl listened as her friends raved about the joys of self-expression, but secretly, innerly, she questioned the whole thing. "There must be more to life than this," she thought. "But what could it be?"

Occasionally she would express her doubts to a friend or a teacher and the reaction would always be the same. They would look at her with a worried expression and then gently suggest that perhaps she should see an art therapist. The young girl learned early on to keep her questions to herself.

Then, one day as she was sitting outside her home, she noticed something unusual. A delicate ray of light was trying to poke through the thick layers of paint that covered her front steps. Curious, the young girl began to chip away at the paint. It was hard work because generations of her ancestors had painted the house many times over. Still, to her growing amazement, the more she chipped, the more the light began to appear.

The girl's heart pounded with excitement. She had read in an ancient book a quaint story about a Creator and his heavenly paint-brush. The young girl now began to suspect that perhaps the old stories might be true after all. She ran to the hardware store and bought a can of paint remover.

When night fell and everyone was asleep, the girl got some rags and went to work. Rubbing, rubbing, patiently and methodically, she slowly began to uncover more and more of the original painting. By daybreak she had scrubbed clean a three-inch area.

The girl sat for a long time and gazed at the light. It was clear that something huge and extraordinary lay hidden beneath these layers of paint and not only under the surface of her house, but under the entire city and the planet as a whole. But it had all been covered over. Every inch of it.

Feelings of grief and despair suddenly overcame the girl as she realized the enormity of the task in front of her. Even if she lived for a thousand years she could never clean all of it. Never. The girl closed her eyes and began to cry.

Then something odd happened. The girl became aware of a pair of lips on her cheek. She was certain that something had just kissed her. The girl opened her eyes. She saw nothing, but a much more intense light was now streaming out of the opening that she had made.

A new and exciting idea occurred to the girl. "I might not be able to clean all of it," she thought. "But if I work real hard I can at lease do my own house!"

Now, filled with new energy, the young girl resumed her rubbing and shipping. She worked all day in full view of her neighbors. Now at first, people were amused by the young girl's behavior. Then, they pitied her. Soon the began to refer to her as "the crazy one."

Of course, none of this stopped the young girl. She was finally happy and for the first time she felt she was doing something useful with her life. "Let others think what they will," she said to herself. "I'm going ahead."

Years passed. The young girl grew up to be a lovely young woman. She had worked nonstop and the front part of her home was almost completely cleansed. A large, shimmering section of the original painting was now clearly visible.

One day a young man approached the house. He had heard about the crazy woman who refused to paint and he wanted to see her for himself. He watched the young woman work from a distance, and then felt himself being drawn closer by the dazzling beauty of the revealed painting. He had never seen anything so beautiful.

The young woman turned around and for a moment, their eyes met. The young man was stunned. The same light that was shining from the painting was also sparkling in her eyes.

Without a word, the young woman offered him a rag and invited him to help. The young man hesitated and then, to his amazement, he found himself on his knees, scrubbing alongside the young woman.

Soon, more and more people began to stop in front of the house. The slowly emerging painting was just too breathtaking to ignore. Painters of all ages became interested in the restoration. A new ideal gripped the people. What if everyone cleaned up their own little part? What would the original painting look like in its entirety?

Slowly, slowly, hundreds and then thousands of ex-painters began to erase the paint from their own front steps. The grim and gloomy planet began to get brighter and brighter and brighter.

Up in heaven, The Creator was joyful. True, it would take a long time for the restoration to be complete, but at last, the work had begun.

Paul Wolff is a screenwriter on the faculty of the U.S.C. School of Cinema and Television. He is also a maggid who leads "Meaning of life" seminars at the Jewish Home for the Aging in Los Angeles, California.

CALL ME ELIE!

I confess to no fixed views about the demography of the *Spiritus Mundi*, but a recent Torah portion led me to wonder whether I'd recognize an angel were I to encounter one. I'm not talking now about the celestial phylum containing, say, Michelle Pfeiffer. I mean an *angel*, a diaphanous messenger like the ones who dropped in unannounced on the likes of the biblical Abraham, Lot, and Hagar, and who, for all we know, might exude garlicky breath or display knobby knees.

Making *aliyah* to Israel, in June 1976, was unquestionably the most pivotal decision of my life, one I have celebrated in many articles and books. Yet there was a juncture when even this true believer came within a deuce of tossing over the whole business. Less than a month after our arrival in Israel as members of *Garin Neot Midbar*, our dream of settling the Negev desert seemed to turn to straw. A whopping majority of our fellow members uncritically acceded to the Jewish Agency's desire that we establish ourselves not in Israel's Negev but rather in the Gaza Strip. "Neot Midbar" would be one bloc of Jewish settlements wedged between the Arab towns of Gaza City and Khan Yunis. This seemed harebrained to us, and very soon my family and several other "Rejectionists" set about organizing an alternative group, one embodying more congenial, to us more high-minded, egalitarian, peace-oriented principles than settling in Arab territory would have entailed.

From our cramped quarters in a Beersheva Immigrant Absorption Center, we set about our quixotic quest for a critical mass of adherents, recruiting in every conceivable corner, even writing to a friend of a distant acquaintance who *might* proceed to

Israel after finishing his Peace Corps stint in Kenya. For a time, such hyperactivity shielded me from considering the tenuousness of our situation.

At the start of the holiday of Sukkot, however, I was felled by the flu. Chills alternated with fever. Never before had I felt so miserable, but physical debility was but a weak echo of my inner turmoil. What perverse imp had led me to forgo our California lives? *What had I done?* Sick, depressed, mired in the Slough of Despond, I lay awake at night contemplating returning to America.

On the evening of the fifth day of Sukkot, my fifth day abed, there came a knock at the door. My wife opened it. The doorway was filled by a bearded man who looked to be in his sixties. He wore hiking boots, khaki shorts, and a beret. He carried a double backpack.

"Ha-im Chertok?" he inquired in a French accent.

I moaned affirmatively. The stranger entered.

"Call me Elie!" he announced. "I am a French Jew traveling around the world. I got your address from Jacques Leiss, an American I met in Kenya. He told me that I could spend the night with you when I reached Beersheva."

Our children, eleven and nine, could not keep from staring at our strange visitor. Offering him a cup of tea, my wife explained that he could not stay with us but that a friend in the Absorption Center had a spare bed in his cubicle.

"*Merci.* Just water hot. I have my own tea."

We all watched as he unlaced and fumbled inside his backpack, emerging with a small packet from which he tapped what appeared to be ground bark into a strainer. He proceeded to filter and sip a reddish brew.

"So," he said at last, "you are, I see, *malade.* If you permit, perhaps I can help you."

I shrugged a listless assent. Elie soon withdrew another packet and brewed a concoction more pungent than the first. Soon I found myself sitting upright at the edge the bed with a towel tented over my head.

"Just breathe," he instructed. "Slowly in, slowly out."

I did as he directed and within minutes the acrid aroma seemed to circulate from nostrils and throat through eyes, head, and the very pores of my skin.

"How do you feel?" he inquired.

"Different," I replied.

"*Bon*. And now the next stage. Have you heard about Chinese needles?"

"Acupuncture?"

"Just so. I learned how to apply the needles from a master in Bangkok."

Once again he fetched something from his remarkable pack: a blue cloth packet that held a variety of needles and a small bottle of alcohol.

Again he busied himself with scalding water at our sink.

"If you will just face away from me and lift your pajama top, I will apply needles at your neck and back. You will feel no pain. In fact, you will feel almost nothing."

By now, I lacked the least inclination to question or resist. For next five minutes, I presented my back to the French stranger with the Chinese needles. As he promised, I felt only the slightest tingling sensation. Ten minutes later he had withdrawn not only his needles, but himself as well, to our friend's cubicle, and I was sound asleep.

Awakening the next morning around seven, not only could I breathe freely, I was ravenous and seemed animated by a surge of energy. Where was Elie?

The backpacker had risen to pray with the 5:30 A.M. *minyan* at a nearby Yemenite synagogue, had returned for his backpack and a cup of tea, and had taken off for parts unknown.

Who or what was that Masked Man with the keen needles and sense of timing? I never saw him again. Nor did I ever hear from the man who apparently sent him, Jack Leiss. But the very day he left, a message arrived from the Jewish Agency. It requested a meeting in Jerusalem to discuss proposals for settling our "peace group" in a small town in the Negev desert called Yeroham—where, indeed, we have lived happily ever since.

....

Haim Chertok, born and raised in the Bronx, made aliyah *in 1976. Since 1988 he has published four books about Israel, the best-known of which is* Stealing Home, *winner of a National Jewish Book Award. His articles appear regularly in the* Jerusalem Post. *He teaches at Ben-Gurion University in Beersheva.*

....

Biker Girl

On the morning before the first seder, I went to my local supermarket to pick up some last-minute items for Passover. Down one of the aisles, a blue-jeaned biker girl stood before the granola bars, concentrating on choice.

She was in her early twenties, with a smooth, inward face. Untamed blonde hair fell onto the black leather of her biker jacket. She wore the jacket open, its straps and silver buckles hanging free, and under it a black sweater tastefully cut to reveal a swell of upper breast. She was striking in appearance and yet there was something self-contained, even modest, about her.

She was, in short, a terrific tough chick.

In an earlier time of my life I might have tried—or at least wondered how I might try—to strike up a conversation with her. Now I merely admired her from afar while attempting to imagine the life out of which she had strolled into my neighborhood supermarket: whose bike she rode the back of, what rooms she ate granola bars in, what the secret fears and hopes of her life might be.

Later, while I was considering egg matzah, I saw her, granola box in hand, find her place in the checkout line. From their perches in neighboring lines, elderly matrons threw her looks considerably less loving than mine. But my admiration for the Biker Girl derived, really, from not so different a source than the sense of threat I read in the eyes of the respectable shoppers. We both recognized her, whether favorably or not, as an icon of freedom.

An icon of freedom on the day before Passover.

I was, of course, concentrating on freedom that morning: the responsible, well-regulated freedom of communal life, freedom by seder, the ordered liberation to which Judaism restricts us. But the Biker Girl seemed onto some larger freedom than that: American freedom, the freedom of the expanding ego inventing itself as it flies.

I did not know, of course, if the Biker Girl was even intelligent, let alone wise, but the knowing grace with which she carried herself suggested to me that she knew something I had forgotten, something about living carefree, like a cat, relaxed and totally alert.

So I compared myself to her in front of our separate displays in the supermarket. She chose granola bars; I chose egg matzah. I did not know what criteria she applied, or how much soul-searching was necessary to her choice, but for me, the simple act of putting a box of egg matzah in my shopping cart on the morning before Passover carried with it the baggage of communal responsibilities and ancient arguments. Even so small an act as buying egg matzah was not quite free for me.

It may seem strange that there could be any weighty issue involving egg matzah, but in my home (or maybe just in my mind), the equivocal freedom of Passover has become entwined in a minor way with the question of whether egg matzah is "permitted."

On the one hand, when I was growing up, we routinely ate egg matzah on Passover—not, to be sure, as the matzah of the seder, but all the rest of the week, slathered with butter, cream cheese, and/or strawberry jam. Even after I had shifted my allegiance to observances more traditional than those of my Reform family of origin, I continued happily to eat egg matzah. On the other, a few years ago, the word began filtering down from Orthodox Headquarters that egg matzah is acceptable on Passover only for the very young, the old, and the sick. It is not chametz, leavened bread—that is, it doesn't treif your dishes—but neither is it fit Passover food for healthy adults.

The rationale for the prohibition of egg matzah, my rabbinic adviser explains to me, is that matzah is meant to be a "poor bread" made of flour and water, while egg matzah, made with eggs and juice, is "enriched bread," a kind of anti-matzah, not chametz, but somehow adulterated—the matzah of compromise, instead of the matzah of freedom.

A lenient minority opinion, however, posits that if you understand egg matzah as cake, it may be okay. That is my view: egg matzah isn't *matzah*, it's dessert or a muffin with dinner. And that was why, after serious thought about Jewish law and the preferences of my family, I dropped two boxes of egg matzah into my cart.

By then, of course, I had lost track of the beautiful Biker Girl. I knew that I would not see her again. Icons of this kind are gifts, like visitations from Elijah the Prophet, who, it is said, roams the world in ordinary guise, appearing when he is needed with a listen for ordinary folk. The Biker Girl was my Lady Elijah, giving me a glimpse into the clarity and freedom of another life.

A freedom you can imagine is one of which you are capable. But there was sadness in all this, too, a longing for that time when I might actually have become the wild and woolly lover of the Biker Girl. Now domesticated, I would have to cultivate the freedom of the mind, the power of metaphor—and I feared I might have trapped myself in arcane speculations about the significance and religious status of egg matzah.

I paid for my egg matzah and went home to prepare the seder. And on the eighth day of the festival, which is a holiday only by rabbinic enactment and thus we are less strict about certain matters, I ate a flat sandwich of buttered egg matzah, thinking of the beautiful Biker Girl.

....

David Margolis is a journalist and novelist. His books include The Stepman *(1996) and* Change of Partners *(1997), both from The Permanent Press. A regular contributor to the* Los Angeles Jewish Journal, *he now makes his home in Israel.*

jumping In

The most exciting story in the Torah is surely the Crossing of the Red Sea. We remember the story from countless Seder-table tellings:

Newly freed from slavery, the Israelites are camped at the shores of the Sea when suddenly the rumbling of Pharaoh's approaching chariots fill the air. Realizing they are trapped, the ex-slaves cry bitterly to Moses, "Were there too few graves in Egypt, that you brought us to die here?!"

Moses prays for deliverance.

"Tell the Israelites to go forward," God directs him. "Lift up your rod and hold out your arm over the sea and split it.. . ."

The rod is lifted, the sea splits, and the Israelites cross in safety. Then they behold the final act of Exodus drama: The sea comes crashing down upon Pharaoh and his armies. As they once drowned Israelite babies in the Nile, so now the Egyptians drown in the Red Sea. The Israelites raise their voices in song. They had been slaves. Their parents grandparents, and great-grandparents, had been slaves. And for all they knew, their children and grandchildren would have been slaves. But suddenly, overnight, freedom: and the promised return to the land of their forefathers.

That's how the Torah tells the story. But when the Rabbis of the Talmud tell it, they add an element. In the manner typical of Midrash, they insert a vignette between the lines:

The people cry out, Moses prays, God commands. But when Moses lifts his rod, nothing happens. He tries again, carefully rehearsing God's words to himself. And again, nothing. Panic wells up within him, he tries, again and again. The sea does not move.

As the beads of perspiration break out on his forehead, the people renew their screams of terror, but Moses is powerless.

And then, suddenly, out of the crowd, comes one man, identified by the Midrash as Nachshon ben Aminadav, a prince of the tribe of Judah. To the astonishment of the people gathered on the shores of the Sea, Nachshon jumps into the water.

"Are you crazy? What are you doing?" his family shouts.

But Nachshon knows exactly what he is doing. He understands, as did no one else, not even Moses, why the sea would not split. He understands that until this moment, all of redemption had been enacted by God: God had sent Moses to Pharaoh, God had sent the plagues that shattered the arrogance of Pharaoh, God had brought His people to the shores of the Sea . . . everything accomplished by God.

But now God was waiting . . . waiting to see if any one, just one, of the Israelites was willing to take a risk for the sake of the promised freedom.

Realizing this, Nachshon jumps in. He wades out until the waters reach his waist. His family's screams fade, and his people stand in silence, watching in wonder. He wades out and the water reaches higher. The water covers his nostrils. And when it reaches the top of his head and his life is in peril, only then does the sea open.

And then he is followed by the rest of the Israelites, who cross in safety.

This story isn't found in the Torah. It was inserted by the Rabbis. As much as they loved the Torah's exodus story, they sensed something was missing. The Rabbis believed that God can only create the conditions for the redemption of the world. But if redemption is truly to come, someone must jump into the water. Someone visionary and brave must be willing to put life on the line and jump into the waters of history to bring the rest of us out of slavery.

In every generation, there are Nachshons willing to jump into the water. Sometimes the water splits, and sometimes it doesn't. But those who have the faith to take the first courageous step redeem the rest of us, still hovering on the shore.

....

Ed Feinstein serves as a rabbi of Valley Beth Shalom in Encino, California, and as a lecturer in the Ziegler School of Rabbinic Studies at the University of Judaism in Los Angeles. His Torah commentaries appear in the Los Angeles Jewish Journal. *Well known for his storytelling, Rabbi Feinstein is reputed to bake the best challach west of the Rio Grande, according to wife Rabbi Nina Feinstein and children Yonah (14), Nessa (11), and Raphael (8).*

....

Dancing on the
Edge of the World

All the world is a very narrow bridge
The point is not to be afraid.
                        —Rabbi Nachman of Bratslav

For years, I had been troubled by my given name. As a child, I had looked up its meaning in a dictionary of names and discovered that "Myra" meant "Sorrow." *Sorrow?* The chubby little girl who had danced in her pink tutu on the front lawn of our house suddenly disappeared. The champion wave-jumper on our strip of Rockaway Beach no longer ran to the ocean. The prankster went underground. From that day on, I felt destined to shlep all the family *sorrows* on my shoulders.

"You're so pretty, but why are your eyes so sad?" my Uncle Abe asked me.

With a name like "Myra," they shouldn't be sad? I wanted to answer.

But I didn't. The mission of my life foreordained by my name stayed my little secret. For years. Years.

When I went to live in Israel, there was, of course, an opportunity to change it. In Israel, Bobs became "Z'evs," Susans became "Shoshanas." I didn't even know how to write "Myra" correctly in vowelless Hebrew; Israelis stumbled over my *mem yod resh aleph:* "Meera"? "Ma'era"? "Mah ya ra" I would say. I might as well have said "Martyr."

Briefly, I tried to run from the name. I went to the Ministry of the Interior in Beersheva when I was thirty, dropped the "R," and Hebraicized my name to "Maya." They duly and approvingly inscribed it as such in my Identity Card. Then I learned that Maya was an acronym for *Milkhemet Yom Ha'Kippur*—the Yom Kippur War—and I wanted none of it. I returned to the Ministry of the Interior and asked for my name back. They said I had to wait seven years.

Seven years later there I was again. The clerk checked my Identity Card. "It's not seven years yet," he mumbled talmudically. "In twenty-four hours, is seven years."

Twenty years later, Maya is still the name inscribed in my Israeli Identity Card. But it is not *my* name anymore.

After returning to live in the States in the heady early years of the Jewish feminist movement, I launched myself in earnest on a journey to find my true name. I tried on "Yasmin." My daughter, then twelve, groaned. A week or so later I met a young woman named "Aden," Hebrew for the paradisal garden of Adam and Eve. *Aden!* I exulted. Happiness! New life! New beginnings! That's it!

"Aden?????" said my daughter. "Mommy, that's *not* your name."

Every other name I tried on got the same reaction.

"I can't seem to find my *true* name," I lamented to a friend. "I don't feel like a 'Myra' anymore. And certainly not a 'Maya.' My Hebrew name as a child was 'Miriyam,' but the rabbis say *that* means 'sorrow' too. *Mar Yam*. Bitter water. Tears . . . who wants it?"

My friend, a Jewish theologian, responded immediately. "The rabbis got it wrong," she insisted. They thought 'Miriyam' means 'bitter water' in the sense of *tears*. But when the Israelites were wandering in the desert, the prophet Miriam was always the one who found the life-giving water. Her name means *salt water*: the water of life, the amniotic fluid, the ocean. . . ."

Her words moved me deeply: my given Hebrew name was *good* after all, inspiring, even ennobling. In my own passion for motherhood and lifelong love of the ocean, I found an ancient kin. My friend had urged me to read the Midrash, and I did. I learned about Miriam's legendary Well which followed the Israelites in their desert wandering, springing up wherever they camped, and sloshing into great rivers on which the Jews of the world sailed to the ocean. The rivers fed by Miriam's Well surrounded a great plain of soft grass on which the homeless and poor slept, fragrant herbs flourished, and miraculous trees bore fruit.

In the months that followed, I planned an experimental spiritual retreat with a circle of women friends: we were eager to try out the new prayers and ceremonies being written by Jewish women around the world. We found an ideal spot: a center where the scents of wild rosemary and night-blooming jasmine seemed to beam us up from San Diego County and land us on the outskirts of Jerusalem, where I had lived for so many years. More than fortuitously, in the field in the back of the retreat center was a narrow, handwrought bridge over a pond of *mayim khayim* / living water, fed by underground springs: nature's very own *mikveh*.

The spot-of-spots for a name-changing ceremony.

The first night of the retreat, as a full moon blazed in the sky, we spiritual *halutznikot* stepped gingerly, one by one, across the narrow bridge. Perhaps it was the precariousness of the bridge. Or the moonlight glistening on the field. Whatever it was, I felt as if to cross the bridge was to step off the edge of the world—into the liberating adventure of creating a new ceremonial territory together. It was at once joyous fun, and holy.

Dramatically draped in the white *galabiyah* of my days camping in the Sinai desert, I spoke about casting off that old "*Sorrow,*" and reassuming the Hebrew name originally given to me. I *loved* the name "Miriyam" now, for with it came the energy of Miriam's *chutpah*, wisdom, loyalty, leadership. "You're worse than the Pharaoh!" she admonished her father when, dreading the edict that would have drowned all Hebrew male babies, he ceased having relations with her mother. "You would destroy the Hebrew girls, too!" I could see her guarding her baby brother as he floated on the Nile, and I laughed with pleasure at her ingenuity in urging the Princess who found his little ark to hire "a Hebrew nurse" to care for him.

And then, when the fleeing Hebrew slaves faced the edge of their old world and miraculously crossed the Red Sea, *Miriam the prophet ... took the timbrels in her hand and all the women went out after her with timbrels and with dances;* I dove deep into the pond three times, and when I emerged, one of the women handed me a tambourine, and we all burst out dancing, drumming, and singing one of the new women's songs:

*And the women dancing with their timbrels
Followed Miriam as she sang her song,
Sing a song to the One whom we've exalted
Miriam and the women danced and danced the
whole night long...
And Miriam the prophet took a timbrel in her hand
And all the women followed her just as she had planned,*

*And Miriam raised her voice in song
She sang with praise and might,
We've just lived through a miracle, we're going to dance tonight.*

And did we ever! On and on, singing, celebrating, dancing like the women at the Red Sea, laughing our old selves off at the edge of our own world that moonlit night.

As I drove into the garage at home after the retreat, my smiling daughter came running up to me.

"I made something for you, Mommy," she said.

She handed me a sheaf of stationery. In simple letters, clear as the day, it read

From the desk of Miriyam.

*The song we sang at the retreat is "Miriam's Song," © Debby Friedman.

.08 ⊙F A SEC⊙∏D

ReshLakesh, then a vagabond and a highway robber, once did an amazing dive which was witnessed by Rabbi Yochanan (who himself was swimming at the time). Rabbi Yochanan declared: "With strength like that you should be studying Torah!"
—Bava Metzia 84a

RABBINICAL SCHOOL, FALL 1997

We've been in rabbinical school for a few weeks now. God is a demanding teacher. *Shacharit* prayers, 7:30–8:30 A.M. *Mishnah* Class, 9:15–10:45 A.M. Hebrew, 11 A.M.–12:15 P.M. Bible, 1–2:30 P.M. *Mincha* prayers, 2:45–3 P.M. *Beit Midrash* study, 3–4:30 P.M. Dinner, 6–7 P.M. Evening class 7–9:30 P.M.

God is merciful. No evening class tonight. Pizza boxes strewn on the floor, we sit in a circle on the carpet of a small apartment. We have come together to share our stories. I am next. I have a hard time explaining to people why I am studying to be rabbi. To people who have known me all my life, I imagine it seems as if I went to Israel a few years ago, saw a bright light, and was transformed into a deeply religious person. To me, though, studying for the rabbinate today is only a natural extension of who I was before: a swimmer.

The obligations of a parent to a son, according to the Talmud, are "to circumcise, redeem, teach him Torah, take a wife for him, and teach him a craft." And, it adds, "to teach him to swim too" (*Kiddushin 29a*). I think I had a medical circumcision in a hospital; I know I wasn't "redeemed," and my scientist dad certainly didn't teach us the biblical *parsha* each week. I'm married now but it wasn't my parents who found my wife. Did mom and dad teach me a craft? Well, I *am* a rabbinical student but I think they'd admit that, if the rabbinate is a "craft," then it's one I chose for myself. On the other hand, my parents *did* teach me to swim.

POTOMAC, MARYLAND—SUMMER 1979

Splat, splat, plop my feet. Puddle, dodge left, head timer, dodge right. It is an art, deck running.

Ileap over the rope and bounce into an oversize lounge chair, wriggling my sweat pants over my wet skin. Tall trees tower over our shady team area. My big chair sinks into muddy grass. It is cool outside. I look up and gaze across the pool at a sign: "Go Potomac!" The letters are written with crumpled newspaper balls stuck into the chain-link fence surrounding our pool.

One of my earliest memories is fearfully gazing through the large windows overlooking the pool at the local JCC while my parents, brother, and sister swam. Though I was too frightened to venture close to the water, my parents persisted in bringing me with them to the pool. It wasn't until my brother and sister came home with ribbons and medals from a swim meet that I decided swimming just might be for me, too. I wasn't good at much else and it sure felt good seeing my name on a First Place ribbon.

"*Daniel! Max! Thomas!* Time to report. *Over here!*"

A booming voice calls me into action. I scramble into my flip-flops and as soon as I hop into place in front of Coach Holden's tall legs, Thomas and Max jump into line next to me.

Holden squats down in between us. At eight years old, we still have to look up to see his face. "Okay guys, your event is being called. Go fast!"

He hands us our cards, stands up, and disappears from view.

Daniel Greyber. Eight-and-under. Twenty-five-meter freestyle. Lane 4.

Dodge left, right. *Splat! Plop!* I jump into the low chair behind lane 4 and clap my knees together. The timers stand in a clump at the other end of the pool. The swimmers from the last race climb out of the pool and the water calms down and starts to shine.

"County record," I whisper to myself as the starter walks toward this end of the pool.

BANG!

I spring off the wall, duck my head under my arms, and do a lean dive down the middle of the lane. My body shudders. The water is like a charge of electricity. I start kicking and spinning my arms at will. When I take a breath, I see arms waving and people jumping through my red tint goggles. Go-go-go-go-go. Kick-kick-kick. Five-four-three-two-one. *Smash.* I hit the wall, hop out of the water, and run to Holden.

"What was my time?"

"16.68."

"Holden, I got a best time! I won."

Holden says nothing to me. He clicks his watch twice. Then he says to the assistant coach, "Max, 23.22. Thomas 25.23."

I try again. "I got a best time!"

Now he looks down. "Daniel, I want to talk to you." He walks away from the team toward the fence.

I follow him away from the crowd. My face feels red.

"What did I do wrong?" I say softly.

He squats down and puts his index finger over his lips. "Shhh. Daniel, you won the race and there's nothing wrong with that. But I want to talk to you about the way you did it. When you win, other people lose, right?"

"Yeah."

"They swim just as hard as you do, right? Just not as fast. Right?"

"Yeah."

"You like it when people say, 'way to go' after you swim, right?"

"Ye-es," I peep.

"When I say 'good job' or 'way to go' I say it for two things."

As if he hears the "huh?" in my mouth, he goes on, "Let me explain. One reason is because you won. But the other is because you tried hard. If you swam a best time but didn't win, I'd still say 'way to go.' So don't you think that everyone who swam the race deserves a handshake or a 'good job'?"

"I guess so."

"Don't be ashamed, little buddy." Holden reaches his long arm around my back and squeezes my shoulder. "You don't have to swim slow. Just remember: I want you to win, but it's not all about getting first. I want you to respect everyone in the water. Just show me you'll remember that next time."

"Okay Holden, you'll be proud of me."

He stood up and messed up my hair. "We're gonna need a great swim out of you for the end relay. Go get'm little guy."

"Here we go Dan-iel, here we go!" APPLAUSE!

"Here we go Dan-iel, here we go!" APPLAUSE!

I curl my toes around the white stone edge of Potomac pool; raise my arms straight out in front of my pudgy tummy, and crouch my legs, ready to spring. My hands are open, palms turned outward, thumbs touching each other. They form a window so I can follow my teammate swimming toward me down the lane.

"Here we go Dan-iel, here we go!"

APPLAUSE!

The window drops lower.

"Go Daniel! You can do it!" my mom yells from behind me.

"Go Daniel, Go Greyber!" screams my dad.

I swing my arms up and over my head like a Ferris wheel and leap off the wall. ICE. Cold charges my body all over. My arms spin through the water. One-two-three-four-five-six-breath right.

"Here we go Dan-iel, here we go!"

One-two-three-four-five-six—I sneak a breath to the right and peak at the splash from the next lane. I can get him! One-two-three-flip turn! I'm at his knees. One-two-three-breath. I'm at his waist. One-two-three-four-breath. I see his shoulders and a mass of waving arms and jumping bodies. I hear a roar—GOOO! Head down. My arms churn the water but my muscles feel heavy and hot. We are head-to-head at the flags. I can do it! I remember Holden's words: "Swim through the wall!" Three-two-one-smash. I hit the wall.

My teammates jump way up in the air. *"Yaaay! Grey-ber! Grey-ber!"* A burst of applause.

First!

I push myself halfway out of the water and, out of the corner of my eye, I see the other boy. I drop back in the water and wait for the other relays to finish.

"Good race."

I reach over the lane rope and shake hands. I climb out and look over to the team area. Standing above the parents and kids is Holden, cheering with two thumbs up. I raise my arms above my head and give him two thumbs up. He lets out a big laugh and yells again, "Way to go, Daniel!" I turn around and join my cheering friends.

We all hope, dream, crave for a moment like that to happen to us. If not in the NBA or the Olympics, maybe the little league game would be enough.

To hear your name chanted.

To come from behind.

To win.

NORTHWESTERN UNIVERSITY, SEPTEMBER 1992

Our team has gathered around a large table in the conference room overlooking the pool. We are big guys, too big for the chairs around the table. We're in jeans and Tee-shirts, itching to get changed. Coach insists: "You can't get somewhere if you don't know where you want to go. I want each of you to have a successful year, but in order to do that, you have to tell me and tell yourselves what that will mean. Before we swim one lap, I want you to write down your goals for this season."

I know coach is right; I need to do this. I've been through this before. Everybody starts out right, getting to bed early, working hard in practice. But after a few months, you're tired of the routine. I know myself. When I hear the clock radio go off at 5:15 A.M. and my muscles still ache from last night's practice, I'll find an excuse to go back to sleep unless I have a clear vision of what I want to accomplish this year.

I close my eyes and lay my head down on the table. I've got to be able to see my goals, to hear them, and taste them. *Grey-ber! Grey-ber!*

APPLAUSE! It's been a long time since a crowd chanted my name. I want that feeling again.

I open my eyes and scribble across the pad: *Anchor the 400 freestyle relay at Big Tens: Win the championship for the team!*

Just one more time, I want to be a hero.

THE POOL, DECEMBER 1992

The metal beams slow to a stop and shift direction. I am lying on my back, sliding back down towards the wall. My feet hit it and I PUSH off again. Underneath me is a towel soaking up sweat from my back. Coach calls it the sled: I lie on a small padded surface that slides up and down on a slanted steel shaft and do hundreds upon hundreds of jumps to strengthen my legs. The grating of metal-on-metal echoes in the emptiness. I close my eyes and play the video in my head. *Grey-ber. APPLAUSE!* My legs are heavy. I am sliding down again. Push off the wall through the water. Drive my legs up and down. My friends have gone home and I am still here. . . . They fear the pressure. I crave it. . . . I glance at the clock. I've done ten minutes more than usual. I stop. The towel is soaked. I can't control the shaking in my legs. I hobble alone toward the locker room to change. The smell of chlorine wafts off the pool and sweat drips off my nose into my mouth. I taste victory.

BIG TEN CONFERENCE SWIMMING CHAMPIONSHIP, FEBRUARY 1993

I stand on a large white starting block high over the pool, my toes rubbing on its gritty surface. Goggle straps wrap snugly into the skin of my smooth, bald head. Clear plastic lenses press tightly around my eyeballs. I look over to the next lane. My opponent is a muscular six-foot-seven shaggy-haired mammoth named Len. He crouches at the edge of the starting block and extends his long fingers across the water, preparing for the relay exchange. I am clearly overmatched.

I stand at the back of the starting block and swing my hands in front of me. Out of the side of my eye, I see the crowd rise in anticipation. My team's deep loud chant floats over the water in front of me:

Here we go Grey-ber, here we go! APPLAUSE!

The air is humid and nervous. The water dances with bright stadium lights. Hard rhythms pulse in my head. I let out something like a growl and feel the power of bubbling anger flow through my toned legs and torso. I expel air forcefully from my chest and swing my arms over my head. As they start to flow forward past my hips I inhale deeply, take two quick steps and leap off the block, soaring high over the water.

There is no youthful innocence, no joy and laughter—every run through the early morning darkness, every push-up and crunch, every moment that makes up a season's worth of work rides on this moment. I know this man only as the Enemy. I pledge every ounce of strength in my soul to beating him.

I hear my mother and father cheering me in my youth. I feel the cradling embrace of my girlfriend at school. I remember the trust of my teammates. I yearn for the passionate beauty of every solitary, lonely athlete and pray for their companionship in this moment. I summon the strength of every failure and redemption; I reach for all of it in order to take down the beast who looms in the next lane. He is Len Rayer, holder of my fears, the obstacle to living a childhood dream, the holder of who I am: the athlete who comes through in the clutch, the hero. . . . I spring off the block and reach for the golden ring.

The first two lengths are perfect. I glide strong and confident. I pull with quick automatic strokes. My body has rehearsed; it runs on autopilot. I am slightly ahead as we enter the second turn. I push off the wall and extend my lead. Rayer makes his move and pulls even just as we head into the third and final turn. The video in my head begins to play. I begin the somersault and . . . am sliding down . . . PUSH! My legs explode powerfully off the wall. I am ahead again. I hear a roar from above the water. *I believe.* The crowd rises to its feet to bear witness. A fierce battle. A struggle of spirits.

I have rehearsed this last length a thousand times. Four strokes, right-left-right-left. *Breathe right.* I see his head behind me at my chest. *I believe.* Four more strokes, right-left-right-left. *Breathe right.* I see his head behind me at my shoulders. *I believe.* Seven strokes to the wall. Right-left-right-left. "*Swim through the wall.*" Right-left and right reach to the wall. The magic moment I have dreamed a thousand times.

Fingertips touch timing pads. Cameras flash. Digits click on the scoreboard display. I rip my goggles off with my left hand. I shift my body around in the water to see the scoreboard at the other end of the pool. My legs churn strongly beneath me. My fist clenches, ready for victory. But God has not seen my video. The number "2" sits next to my name. Len Rayer has touched me out by eight one-hundredths of a second and I am sliding down . . . down.

I drape back in the water and stare at the ceiling. The beams are still. I sink slowly beneath the surface. The waters envelop my chest, my shoulders, my eyes. Len Rayer can only hold his right hand up in the air as his teammates slap it and jump in jubilation on the deck above. My right hand has found the rope. His left hand rests on it. Both lay lifeless on the lane rope that divides us. I cling with my left hand to the deck above. Len Rayer has been taken to the limit, spent of everything. He is barely able to mutter "nice race." The sound echoes between us. The spotlight does not shine in our cave of dark exhaustion. We struggle to climb from the pool, to return to the world from a hellish descent, tumbling with our fears and hearts and dreams intertwined. We shake hands but there is only one winner.

I fall into the warm down pool, stunned. Too stunned to slap in anger at the pool. Too paralyzed to scream under water in frustration. A dream ripped from my grasp. I collapse into a pit of my fears, reeling without a hold. Choke. Nice guy. Loser. "I want you to win, but it's not all about getting first. I want you to respect everyone in the water." Holden's words sat spurned, ignored, in a distant part of my mind. We shake hands.

I had learned to respect others. But there is only one winner. I had not learned to respect myself.

WORLD MACCABIAH GAMES, SUMMER 1993

I sit on the carpet at the foot of my bed in the Goldar Hotel. My roommate is a tall and lanky, blond Californian named Dan. We are both seeded first for our events tonight at the Maccabiah finals. Familiar butterflies float on the soft light of mid-afternoon and settle comfortably to dance in the pit of our stomachs. Old questions haunt me: Would I win the big race or would I choke? Would I come through in the clutch? Am I a winner? A loser? On other afternoons like this, fear has consumed me. Yet today Dan and I are able to stretch and talk, and even laugh. Fear still looms in the dark corners of our selves, because fears do not change; we do.

The experience at Big Tens had changed me. After I lost to Len Rayer, I had fallen into the warm down pool, sunk twenty feet to the bottom, laid down as if on a bed, and had closed my eyes. I had felt as if swimming had cast me out of itself.

How strange then that that night, deep on the pool floor, I had felt my soul rising to the surface, floating high above the sport. I had yearned to fly to the heavens, but maybe I had asked more of the pool than it had to give. Swimming had given me glorious, white-hot, promethean moments, moments that masked themselves in the divine. But those moments were ultimately only a shadow of what I yearned for. I had yearned for ultimate meaning.

We all need a sense of the divine in our lives, a sense that what we do on a day-to-day basis has ultimate importance. Though I didn't know it at the time, losing to Len Rayer was a blessing. The cheer of the crowd had become my idol. If I had won, I might have spent many years or even a whole lifetime pursuing ultimate fulfillment in the gleaming moments of sports. When I lost, I learned that I am worth more than cheer of the crowd, the adulation of teammates. Finally I saw myself as more than a swimmer, more than a teammate, more than the person I thought myself to be.

God has many names. Perhaps one of them is "More Than."

I warm up for a while in the Tel Aviv pool and then spend time talking with my mom and my uncle and aunt and cousin who have come to see me swim. I sit with the U.S. team and cheer on my teammates. My race approaches. I walk to the starting area, say a prayer, and prepare for the start.

"In lane 4 from the United States, Daniel Greyber. . ."

I remember very little of the race now. It went well, and as I reached back for the wall, there was no hush in anticipation for the results. I had won by plenty. I pumped my fist in the air and looked toward my team and family and the Hebrew signs of Israel. I leaned back in the water and let the sun soothe my soul; somehow, I felt at home. I shook hands with my opponents and climbed out of the pool into the warm evening air. As I hugged my teammates and embraced my family, I also knew that even if I had lost, it would have been OK.

Daniel Greyber is a rabbinic student at the Ziegler School of Rabbinic Studies at the University of Judaism in Los Angeles. He helped to found and direct "Lishma," an egalitarian yeshiva-study summer program at Camp Ramah in California. He is married to Jennifer and is the proud father of Alon Meir, who was born while Daniel was writing this story.

İf the Wisdom You Have is Never Expressed in Deeds

If the wisdom you have is never expressed in deeds, you become like a juniper tree in the wilderness. The juniper has many branches, but its roots are weak. When a strong desert wind blows, the tree is easily uprooted. It can topple over on its face.

But when your deeds are greater even than your wisdom, you are like a tree which may lack branches but which surely has strong roots. Though all the winds of the world furiously blow it, it doesn't stir. It is like a tree planted by the water whose roots spread out to the riverbank. Even in the hottest weather, its leaves are green. Even in a drought, it bears fruit.

Rabbi Eliezar ben Azariah, from Pirke Avot: Sayings of the Fathers

SAMUEL M. STAHL

On Micah and Menschlekeit

In the era of the First Temple, when Jerusalem was threatened by Assyrian attack, the prophet Micah warned the people that if they did not change their ways they would be destroyed.

Whatbehavior so outraged Micah? It was not the peoples' failure to observe religious ritual, for with great fidelity they appeared at the Temple on all the festivals to offer their top-quality animal sacrifices in abundance. But those sacrifices meant little to Micah, for in his eyes they and their leaders were morally corrupt. Micah challenged them: How should we truly serve God?

Often quoted by American politicians, the classic translation of Micah's answer is *It has been told thee, O Man, what is good, and what the Lord requires of thee: only to do justly, and to love mercy, and to walk humbly with thy God.*

The first phrase of that translation, though, is grammatically inaccurate. It should be *Human beings have told you what is good, but what does God require of you?* In other words, human beings may claim that God demands that we perform religious rituals, but what God truly desires—indeed, *requires*—of us is ethical behavior. The prophet Micah insists that while we are not exempt from the practice of ritual, the vital expression of religious behavior is *menschlekeit*, treating one another humanely.

A few days before Passover, the late Rabbi Israel Salanter, founder of the ethics-based Musar movement in eastern Europe, gathered together a group of his students. He was about to send them out to inspect a local matzo-baking factory to certify that its products were indeed "Kosher for Passover."

"Rabbi, is there something we should particularly look for there?" one of his students asked.

"Yes, definitely," said Rabbi Salanter. "When you get to the factory, you'll see an old woman baking matzo. The woman is poor and has a large family to support. Make sure the owners are paying her a living wage."

....

Samuel M. Stahl is Rabbi of Temple Beth-El in San Antonio, Texas. He is the author of Making the Timeless Timely: Thoughts and Reflections of a Contemporary Reform Rabbi *(Nortex Press, 1993). This story was adapted from a commentary in his "Learn Torah With," vol. 3, number 40 (Shabbat, July 19, 1997),* © *Torah Aura Productions.*

RABBI AKIVA

....

EVERYTHING IS FORESEEN...

Everything is foreseen—yet human beings have freedom of choice. The world is judged by grace, yet everything depends on the nature of your deeds.

Rabbi Akiva, Sayings of the Fathers

Paying Attention

"You were a missionary child," my mother told me on a recent visit. We agreed that my life had been a quest to discover my calling and it was a blessing that I had finally found it. "Better late than never," we nodded in unison. The many wrong twists and turns I had taken in the process were remembered but unsaid.

Fifteen years prior to this conversation, my life had crashed. I was unemployed, homeless, practically penniless, and out of new ideas. My only child had departed for college and empty nest felt better than no nest. I had left social work five years before to pursue Success—and had been a failure. I had tried it all and I was tired of it all.

In the quest for success, I read *Think & Grow Rich*, and began to study Science of Mind, a metaphysical religion. I failed all their Creative Visualization seminars because I didn't know what to visualize. Before I killed myself I called the Science of Mind's "Expect a Miracle" practitioner. I requested an audience.

"What do you want?" she asked me when we met.

"I don't know," I whined. "If I knew, I'd go get it." Then I added, "What I want is to know what I want."

"Do you pray?" she asked me.

"Of course not," I answered quickly. "I'm an intellectual and an atheist. I'm a cultural Jew but I've never believed in prayer."

"Close your eyes," she said, "and take my hand. Father of the Universe, take this woman by the hand and guide her to her rightful work. She knows she wants to do something important and meaningful but she doesn't know what it is. That's it," she said. "You don't have to do anything special. Just pay attention."

I felt sort of silly when I left her office that Thursday afternoon. That Sunday, I opened the *L.A.Times* Classified section, as usual, to the Sales & Marketing section. But then I heard an inner voice whisper, "I wonder what Social Work has to offer."

There it was. The smallest ad in the social work column, but it jumped right out at me:

Person of Jewish background and culture to work with Jewish criminal offenders. MSW required. Apply at Gateways Hospital.

The hairs on my arms stood up. I was flooded with an unfamiliar sensation that today I know to be AWE.

"Oh my God," I said. "This stuff works!"

At that moment, I made a conscious decision to call what had happened Divine Guidance rather than just Coincidence. That decision of faith was to transform my existence.

I got the job, of course. I had always been attracted to outlaws and had long had fantasies of being some Clyde's Bonnie. I was thrilled to know that there were Jewish bad boys and girls. I couldn't wait to get into those jails and talk to those Jewish criminals.

"Wait till my mother hears this one," I smirked. I knew I had found my mission.

My first day on the job I was taken to Sybil Brand, the L.A. County Jail for Women. I submitted my "Inmate Visitor" slips for women who had asked to see a Rabbi or who had been identified for me by "Bubbe Theresa, the Jewish Jail Lady," the amazing woman whose mission it is to cull Jewish names from the County Jail computer printout, and who, at 87, has been finding Jews in jail for over 50 years, and making sure they receive religious and social services from the time they are arrested until their release from custody.

I sat on the visitor side of the partition and awaited my first inmate. She was a forty-five-year-old woman I will call "Sheila Blum." A deputy motioned to Sheila to sit across from me. She was wearing a red shmata with COUNTY JAIL stamped across her back and she was missing a few teeth. She had no idea why she had been summoned to the attorney room for a visit.

I introduced myself as the social worker from the Jewish Committee for Personal Service, who had come to help her change her life if she wanted to. She started to cry. Within ten minutes, we were connected as two women with eerily similar life stories. A graduate of Hunter College, Sheila had been a high school English teacher until her escalating heroin habit forced her to sell drugs for a living. She had a grown daughter, the same age as my daughter, who refused to see her unless she agreed to go to rehab. The husband who had turned her on to drugs when he returned from Vietnam had died of an overdose. She was facing a state prison term.

The more we talked, the more powerfully I realized that I could have been sitting where Sheila was, but for the Grace of God. As the steel doors clicked open to let me out that afternoon, I felt what my immigrant ancestors must have felt when they reached the shores of freedom and kissed the ground in gratitude. Still, I couldn't wait to get back in. I yearned to help Sheila find the "courage to change," and I was eager to meet the other Jews in jail and hear their stories.

I was hooked!

Day after day, I met compelling, extreme, beguiling, and incomprehensible men and women who were completely disconnected from themselves. Their spiritual *corpus collasum* was severed. Intention had no connection to action; self, no connection to self-image. Their choices contradicted their values.

But the truth was that they mirrored my own split, as I learned to love and despise them simultaneously. I fell in love with Barney, a Brooklyn college boy who listened to Bach, read Krishnamurti, meditated, shot heroin, and robbed banks. We shared a passion for Jackie Robinson, a belief in the innocence of Ethel and Julius Rosenberg, and we had both contemplated suicide for the same reasons.

I fell in love with Annie, a seventy-seven-year-old woman who conned the bank out of $500,000 so she could buy Ronald Reagan's house in Malibu. . . "A president's house," she said, "I wanted to leave it to my grandchildren." Every time I visited her in County Jail and then later in State Prison, her hair was done and her nails were polished. I was in awe that she would bother.

"I'm not going to let myself go just because I'm in here," she said. "It's better than a nursing home!"

I met a talmudic scholar and respected physician who shot his ex-wife in front of their children; a pious Jew who infected his six-year-old daughter with gonorrhea; and a compulsive gambler who devotedly nursed his dying grandfather and then stole his stamp collection to pay the bookie.

They were all addicts of one kind or another. Through them, I began to see addiction as a spiritual dis-ease — an inability to unify the self. For them, the self was experienced as an inner emptiness, a deep dark hole they tried to fill with substances and/or desperate action that numbed the ache. They were trapped in an addictive cycle, chasing the illusion of wholeness, which they experienced only while *in pursuit* of their particular "fix," whether it was drugs, alcohol, sex, food, gambling. Once they "scored," though, the downward cycle erupted again, and they were overcome by shame and guilt. When the cycle hit its nadir, they made resolutions to themselves and promises to others — resolutions that they violated as soon as the craving to fill the void, the craving for that sensation of wholeness, overpowered their good intentions yet again. They were tormented themselves and tortured the people who loved and cared for them. Only jail or death released them from the addictive trap.

I soon began to see the same people, who had sworn they would never return to jail, land up behind bars again within months of their release. They had gone back to the same people and the same situations that were part of their addictive lifestyle, had "fallen off the wagon" within hours.

If only there was a place they could go to from jail or prison to recover from the cycle of addiction. I knew such a place would have to be spiritual and have to be Jewish and have to be a home, not an institution. I began to do research, and discovered Dr. Abraham Twerski's article, "Judaism and the Twelve Steps" in the collection *Addictions in the Jewish Community*. My reading of that landmark article, connecting the Twelve Steps of Alcoholics Anonymous and Torah, gave birth to the idea of Beit T'shuvah. I envisioned Beit T'shuvah, whose name means at once "The House of Return,"

"The House of Repentance," and "The House of Response," as a warm and loving Jewish home with an open kitchen, where Jewish addicts and criminals would become whole through a blend of Torah, the Twelve Steps, and the Truth.

I knew that the teachers would have to be people who had been there, people who could serve as spiritual guides and role models, not "professionals" whose training and education had taught them to hide their own imperfections. The timing was good. The growing problem of homelessness had generated a large pot of money to establish shelters for the homeless. I submitted a grant to buy a home.

In March 1987, with a grant from the Federal government to establish a homeless shelter for Jewish men and women coming out of jails and prisons, Beit T'shuvah opened its doors. I was the only staff. I turned to the Recovery and the Jewish communities for help. I found "L'Chaim," a Jewish recovery community in Los Angeles, and the "JACS" in New York. And in the state prison, I found a Torah teacher.

Mark Borovitz was a two-time loser and bad-check writer who was serving as the Rabbi's inmate clerk at the California Institution for Men at Chino. Spokesman for the prison's Jewish congregation, he invited me to a meeting in order to tell me what the men needed when they got out. I found Mark arrogant and abrasive.

"If you're so smart," I challenged him, "when you get out of here, why don't you come and help me?" And one day not too long after that, he showed up.

"I'm here to help," he said.

"A man who walks his talk at last!" I said to myself, and I hired Mark as my administrative assistant.

Since that time, Mark has helped both Beit T'shuvah and me grow in ways I hadn't even imagined. He had the chutzpah I lacked, a passion for Jewish learning and teaching, and a God-given gift to know and to touch the souls of others. He lived his own t'shuvah out loud, revealing his sins and his *Return* to God through Torah. He understood that the essence of t'shuvah is the conversion of "the evil inclination," what the ancient sages call *yetzer ha'rah*, to Divine

Service, and he applied his persuasive powers to convince Rabbis, teachers, and community leaders that kids would (and should) listen to him. He became a Hebrew School teacher, a popular public speaker, and the spiritual leader of the Beit T'shuvah Community.

In the summer of 2000, he will be ordained as a Rabbi, and we will celebrate our tenth wedding anniversary.

Today there are twenty-five men and twelve women in the Beit T'shuvah Community. We resemble a large, fairly traditional, Jewish family. Mark is the archetypal Patriarch whose penetrating gaze sees both the shmutz and the purity of your soul and will go *to any lengths* to convert you to 51 percent decency. He gets up every morning at 4 A.M. and before he goes to school, he teaches Torah to the Men's House at 6 A.M., and to the women at 7 A.M. They've told him that when they begin the day with Torah they have a better day.

And I am Mother, willing to give you the benefit of the doubt, erring on the side of kindness and mercy. We fight over what is best for the men and women of Beit T'shuvah, and struggle together to teach each one according to his or her own way. The residents may get mad at either or both of us, but they never accuse us of hypocrisy or lack of concern. For they know our souls as well as we know theirs. Together with the discipline of a spiritual path, this mutual baring and touching of souls has seemed to support healing and the quest for wholeness; damaged people become able to *return* to themselves, to their families, and to God. Last year we had three marriages, two *brises*, several college graduations, and a few deaths. Many members of our Family come "home" on *erev Shabbat*, Friday night, to celebrate their life cycle and sobriety events at our services.

The stories that they tell inspire all of us to continue to pay attention.

Harriet Rossetto, L.C.S.W. is the Executive Director of Gateways Beit T'Shuvah. She is a therapist, writer, and lecturer specializing in issues of addiction, family, and spirituality. She is married to Mark Borovitz, Rabbi of the Beit T'shuva community.

THE BROKEN TABLETS

The broken tablets were also carried in an ark.
Insofar as they represented everything shattered
everything lost, they were the law of broken things,
the leaf torn from the stem in a storm, a cheek touched
in fondness once but now the name forgotten.
How they must have rumbled, clattered on the way
even carried so carefully through the wasteland,
how they must have rattled around until the pieces
broken into pieces, the edges softened
crumbling, dust collected at the bottom of the ark
ghosts of old letters, old laws. Insofar
as a law broken is still remembered
these laws were obeyed. And insofar as memory
preserves the pattern of broken things
these bits of stone were preserved
through many journeys and ruined days
even, they say, into the promised land.

Rodger Kamenetz is a poet and writer, author of The Jew in the
Lotus, Stalking Elijah, Terra Infirma, *and* The Missing Jew: New
and Selected Poems. *He lives in New Orleans and is on-line at*
http://www.literati.net/Kamenetz.

....

GOD'S HOUSE

When Jim Wallis, Evangelical minister and editor of the widely read Christian monthly *Sojourners,* called me to join sixty other religious leaders in Washington, D.C., at a protest of President Clinton's dismantling of welfare, he didn't tell me how spiritually rewarding it would be. It had been a long time since the last time I had been arrested, and that time had not been fun at all. I had been a professor of philosophy at the University of Washington in Seattle and an organizer of antiwar demonstrations when I was indicted as one of the "Seattle Seven" and arrested as I drove from the university parking lot.

Months later, when I sat in prison at Terminal Island Federal Penitentiary in Long Beach, California, I looked forward to Hanukkah as a moment to reconnect with the joy of our Jewish liberation tradition. As it turned out, every other Jewish prisoner shared that anticipation. But after we sang a few songs at the Hanukkah service, the chaplain broke the news which he thought would thrill us: permitted by the authorities to bring only two items into the prison, he had brought kosher salami and bologna, rather than a menorah and Hanukkah candles. Few of the prisoners were cheered. Though the food was terrible in prison, delicatessen was no substitute for the spiritual high and comforting memories we sought through the lighting of candles. It seemed to me then that so many Jews were turned off Judaism precisely because they had been fed salami instead of spirit in the synagogues of their youth.

What a joy, then, in the ensuing years to connect with other young Jews in the Havurah movement and then in Jewish Renewal. The Freedom Seders and the Hanukkah celebrations affirming the link between the Jewish struggles for liberation and those of others in the States and the world; the religious services, rich with the voices of women and alive with a Hasidic fervor; the joy of Shabbat infused with the music of Shlomo Carlebach: all bespoke a new kind of Jewish energy that was as infectiously seductive, liberating, and delicious.

Yet as our new movement grew, so too had a religious right in America. It was dominating public discourse with its own definitions of what God required. Theirs was a punishing and harsh vision—a movement using religious language to support homophobia and patriarchal assumptions. In response, preexisting prejudices against religion among America's liberal intellectuals and social-change activists intensified. As the founder of *Tikkun* magazine, I was in a daily quandary: those who might have loved the magazine for being a Jewish voice supporting progressive politics were nevertheless also deeply suspicious of *Tikkun* because of our unequivocal support for God and Shabbat and Jewish religious practice. Religion had become so clearly identified with the religious right that most liberal Jews seemed to believe that spirituality was a step on a slippery slope to political reaction. Renewal Jews, on the other hand, some of them veterans of the antiwar and freedom struggles of the sixties and seventies, wanted to keep their distance from anything "political," imagining that they'd be tainted and dragged down into an unloving muck. Committed to a political liberation that was also a liberation of the spirit, I tried to disidentify *Tikkun*'s version of the "politics of meaning" from the politics of the religious right.

Imagine my trepidation to be called by a group of Evangelical Christians. I soon realized, though, that these were Evangelicals who were standing up for the rights of the poor, not using the bible to champion the prejudices of the powerful. In fact, the sixty Evangelical ministers I soon found myself among, took the Bible's injunctions to "seek justice" just as seriously as the committed secular progressive Jews I knew.

So it was with Bible in hand that sixty-one of us entered the Capitol rotunda to begin our nonviolent civil disobedience in protest against the cuts in funding to the poor and vulnerable. One after another of us read passages from the Prophets—and was arrested and removed from the rotunda. The police handcuffed us, put us into a large police bus, drove us to a nearby police station, and then, mysteriously, left. We sat for hours. We began to sing; feeling that we had been given this wonderful moment to serve God's will, I taught the sixty ministers the song of the psalmist's plea, *Pitchu lee sha'arei tsedek / Avo bom, ohdeh yah /* "Open the gates of justice for me that I may enter to thank God." Soon the bus rocked with energy; together we sang Reb Shlomo Carlebach's *niggun,* his wordless melody.

The moment transcended political prejudices—on both sides. Ministers spoke of their frustration with the Jewish community's fierce desire to keep religious values out of the public sphere. Couldn't Jews see, they asked me, how badly America was suffering from a crisis of materialism and selfishness? I shared my understanding of the legitimate fears our Jewish world felt at having a religious Christianity shoved down our throats the moment the gates opened to spiritual issues in the public sphere. I told them how much I had hated being forced to say "The Lord's Prayer" in school—both because it felt like an imposition by the majority culture and because the rote recitation had nothing to do with the spiritual energies I felt when praying.

Spiritual energies? That was something they could relate to. One after another told me that every political Jew they had ever met had been resolutely secular, unable to see any connection between their politics and God, and visibly distrustful of those who used God language. And every religious Jew they had ever met justified the oppression of Palestinians and seemed relatively uninterested in the plight of the poor.

Well, I told them, the same kind of misperceptions existed in the Jewish world about religious Christians. Very few of us in the Jewish world had ever met a Bible-quoting Evangelical who was willing to put their bodies on the line for the sake of the poor. Most of us suspected that the word *Evangelical* meant "right-wing." No, they told me, there was a growing movement of social justice–oriented

Christians. Sure, I acknowledged, there had been a powerful group of leftie Catholics who opposed war. No, they told me, it was not just the Catholic left—there were also Christians in the Protestant evangelical movement, and they were beginning to organize themselves. But surely, they asked me, wouldn't the Jewish community be the hardest nut to crack, given its fears of religion in the public sphere?

Well, yes—I too feared religion in the public sphere, if it was going to be an insistence that the "religion" be Christianity. I didn't want Jesus imposed on me or on anyone else. But I did want a new kind of spirituality to be introduced into the public sphere, a spirituality which taught the value of love, caring, solidarity, gratitude, thanksgiving, awe, and wonder. These were the values at the heart of what I was calling a "politics of meaning."

For many of the Evangelicals on that bus, the notion of religious values without Jesus was a hard step to take. But for many more, the hours of discussion began to open a new gate of consciousness. As I talked to them about the religious and social visions of many Jewish Renewal leaders, the ministers became more aware that their vision of serving God had to be expanded. What would "serving God" come to mean for them, if the "God" served weren't only Christian?

Perhaps, some said, it was time for a Christian Renewal as well, and even a national Call to Renewal for all faiths.

Four hours had passed. The police reentered the bus and told us we were about to be booked. And then an amazing thing happened. Spontaneously, the entire bus rocked with the rousing song of the psalmist: *Pitchu lee sha'arei tsedek, Avo bom, ohdeh Yah: Open the gates of justice for me, that I may enter to thank God.* As we sang, I tasted what the prophet meant when he heard the voice of God proclaim, "*My house shall be a house of all peoples,*" for the police bus had been transformed into a place of worship, into God's house. I experienced the pleasure of being with Christians without being apologetic or chauvinistic: to be, instead, comrades searching together for a way to share God's house and make it a house for all people.

....

Michael Lerner is editor of Tikkun: A BiMonthly Jewish Critique of
Politics, Culture and Society; *and author of* Jewish Renewal: A Path
to Healing and Transformation *(HarperCollins, 1995),* The Politics
of Meaning: Restoring Hope and Possibility in an Age of Cynicism
(Perseus/AddisonWesley, 1996), and, with Cornel West, Jews and
Blacks *(NAL Dutton,1996). He is rabbi of Beyt Tikkun synagogue
in San Francisco.*

WHO IS WISE?

Who is wise? The person who learns from all people . . . Who is mighty? Those who are able to discipline their passions . . . Who is rich? Those who rejoice in the portion given them . . . Who is worthy of honor? Those who respect all human beings.

Rabbi Shimon ben Zoma, Sayings of the Fathers

THE WALLET AND THE
COLD TOE

In the days before the Jewish calendar was fixed, a committee convened every autumn to decide whether to add a "leap month" to the lunar year so that the Passover festival would fall not in the winter, but in the spring.

The Talmud asks why the King and the High Priest, the two most obviously important leaders of the people, were forbidden to join that committee.

And it explains: Though the King collected taxes once a year, he paid his soldiers and civil servants once a month. He thus had a built-in incentive to say "no" to extending the year, for if the leap month was added, his treasurer would have to cut an extra payroll check.

As for the High Priest, every year he had to prepare in a special way for the Yom Kippur ritual he was obligated to perform. After changing his clothing, he was required to immerse himself in a ritual bath five times. But the High Priest never wore shoes, and the floor of the Temple was made of stone. If it was cold, he could warm the ritual bath, but afterwards, he would still have to step barefoot onto the stone floor. Adding the leap month to the calendar would make Yom Kippur fall a month later—when the floor would be even colder.

Does the Talmud mean to tell us that the King would argue at the committee meeting that adding a leap month would drain his treasury? that the High Priest would appeal to the committee on behalf of his chilled big toe?

Or is the Talmud suggesting that when the committee convened, the King and High Priest would in all likelihood weave elaborate and subtle arguments against adding the month? that their passionate words would fall on their listeners' ears ringing with truth and fairness? that on behalf of shortening the year, they would appeal to the finest ideals, the keenest senses, the most noble emotions, of their fellow committee members?

That, bedazzled by their learning and logic, no one at the meeting would know that it was the wallet and the cold toe that were driving the eloquent arguments of the mouth. . . .

Label Lam is a rabbi in Monsey, New York, involved in Jewish Outreach education. He occasionally writes for DvarTorah@Torah.org, by Project Genesis, from which this excerpt is taken (www.torah.org).

THE JEWISH BITE

"You're not a Jew, you're a Communist."

These loving words were uttered by my father during my first year at UC Berkeley. For him, my thriving interest in politics and my seeming disinterest in religion were connected. Though he spoke in jest, five years later I'm still mulling over his words. No, I'm not a Communist—but just how Jewish am I?

In our family, my father has always been the professional Jew. He goes to services every weekend, and our home overflows with Jewish books—from philosophical explorations of the Hebrew Bible to ethnic toilet humor—if there's a Jew in there, Dad knows it front to back. Come to think of it, my father becomes more religious as the years go by. Lately, he's been attending weekend spiritual retreats with other Jews, leading services at his Sephardic temple, and in our own home, becoming the Mariah Carey of Friday night prayer: he indulges each word far past its original syllabic value.

My other family members are far less devout, but nevertheless have considered me the black sheep where religion is concerned. This is a recent occurrence; when I was young, I was far more open. I have vivid recollections of family holidays, perhaps because they differ only slightly from those today: the whole family milling around our house, platters of wonderfully fatty foods, everyone screaming to make their voices heard, fights, spills, laughter, politics, wild gesticulation, and lots of kisses. My grandmother adoringly fattens us up, my uncle baits my sister and I with chauvinistic jokes, and my mother rushes to and from the table immersed in Hostess mode, carefully balancing efficiency with charm.

But in the olden days, I had a ritual of my own. As a child, I would sneak into the bathroom to talk to God. Sometimes I would include a prologue of gratitude, vaguely sensing that I was supposed to thank "Him" for my health and my family. Other times, I would cut right to the chase and ask for favors—a new Barbie doll, a sign of affection from beloved fellow third-grader Clinton, or simply the promise of a life full of happiness. Even then, though, the relationship (with God, not Clinton) was tenuous. My fervent desire to believe was combined with an innate sense of skepticism. Often my prayers would begin with a "Look, if you're actually there, then . . ." or "Okay, you're either not there or too busy to take time out for me but I wondered if. . . ." The point was not to determine whether a higher power actually existed. Rather, the point was the possible clarity I could find while sitting on the toilet and hoping my words mattered to someone or something.

The habit dwindled when I hit my teenage years. First, I found I loved existentialism, and writers like Sartre struck a chord with me in a way religion did not. Religion seemed only to manifest an embarrassing and desperate desire to know the Unknowable, thinly veiled as Objective truth. It betrayed a sort of weakness, and that frightened me. I was also averse to anything that encouraged complacency. Phrases like "The Lord works in mysterious ways" disgusted me, as if there were any rationalization possible for the ignominious history of the human race—slavery, misogyny, cruelty. Besides, my increasingly feminist sensibility had obliterated my old Santa Clausian model of God: wisdom and truth embodied by a bearded white male, fleshy, friendly, and firm. With patriarchy effectively intellectually dismantled, God was like the Wizard of Oz, an insecure little guy with a megaphone. To this day, though, my family shudders if I say, "I don't believe in God." Even writing those words down, I'm frightened. I don't want to be struck down by lightning. I don't want others to shudder.

But it is nearly impossible for me to reconcile the beauty and richness of the Jewish tradition with my increasingly postmodern self. In the world of academia, from which I have just emerged, objectivity is a dying concept. TRUTH has exploded into relativity, subjectivity, plurality. Nothing is black-and-white, and the desire to know something absolutely is unhealthy residue from primordial Electra/Oedipal complexes. How can my "self" be Jewish if the very concept of selfhood is being exploded? I graduated from college in a state of existential crisis and confusion, and I figure these states are the most fertile grounds for growth. To challenge, to think critically, to subvert, disrupt, engage: these are valuable tools.

Yet it occurs to me, now that I am out in the world, that these are also very *Jewish* tools. Searching for meaning, rejecting simplicity in favor of complexity: such actions have long suited our tribe. And no matter what critical theory or philosophy I espouse, no matter if I spend holidays at services or not, or whether I regard the Bible as a piece of literature, the golden nugget of Jewish culture still gleams within.

For I find that all of my best friends wind up being Jewish. They are warm, extroverted, passionate, intellectual, and strong-willed. Coincidence? I'm not so sure.

I find that many of my biggest romantic crushes are on Jews. They are men whose intelligence and sensitivity mingle with a very appealing sense of irony.

Few (appealing) people can suffer innumerable wrongs and survive without a sense of humor. But that sense of humor has a little bite in it for Jews. Jews, I notice, really dig irony.

We are, of course, not the only tribe that has ever survived atrocities with brilliance and humor. We have a natural affinity with all underdogs, as I see it. And this last year has taught me that the spirit of the underdog can be very useful indeed.

Nine months ago, I suffered a serious back injury which put me in unyielding daily pain, a pain which makes nine months feel like nine decades. It's hard, sometimes, to believe that I will heal, that I will be "normal" again one day soon. Some days I wallow in self-righteous self-pity. Sometimes I cry on and off all day. But at the end of the day, I find that I force myself to stop feeling so victimized and get off my inflamed ass.

I'm convinced that it's the little Jew in me that makes that possible.

We're tough cookies, us Jews. We don't take much lying down. It's hard to quiet or discourage us. No matter what the obstacle, somehow, we forge on. We've survived the unthinkable and dared to rise up from the ash.

In other words, we've got backbone.

Which helps.

Ilyse Mimoun graduated from UC Berkeley in 1999, where she focused on Women's Studies and Dramatic Art. She is now an actor and writer living in Los Angeles.

Nondenominational Soup: or, The Making of a Jewish Joke

Humor, I have found, is a formidable tool. With it, a craftsman of words can wield a powerful weapon over his enemies, his students, and peers. The Jewish joke in particular caught Freud's eye, for he saw in it a sophisticated way to disarm a bigot by making himself appear to be the butt of the joke. Groucho Marx, too, used a classic example of that form in the punch line everyone knows: *I would never join a club that would have me for a member.* In a time when country clubs excluded blacks and Jews, Marx turned the bigot unwittingly against himself. On one level, what self-respecting Jew would join a club that discriminated against Jews? But the bigot hears something else: "You see," he says, "even Jews don't like being around Jews!" There is nothing to attack. The Jew has stabbed himself, he thinks, and so the bigot walks away, albeit somewhat confused.

Because humor is infectious, many have learned to shroud sage advice in its cloak, where the truth behind the joke may be discerned only by the careful listener.

Once upon a time, there was a rabbi beloved throughout the Pale for his compassion and generosity. One day, his neighbor, the local butcher, brought him a gift of a chicken, and so the rabbi insisted that he stay and enjoy the meal.

"Rabbi, I would love to, but I can't," said the butcher."My only brother is waiting outside, and *has v'halila* I should leave him alone."

"So invite him in, too," said the rabbi. "With such a chicken, there will be plenty of soup for all!"

But the butcher's brother also declined. "Thank you, but no thank you, Rabbi," he said. "My wife is at home waiting for me to return."

"Well then, invite your wife!" the rabbi pleaded, "for this kindness must be repaid."

The next day, a woman knocked on the rabbi's door and said that she was the sister of the wife of the husband whose brother had brought the chicken. The rabbi sighed, but invited her in and offered her some broth from the soup.

The news of the rabbi's generosity spread rapidly through the town. Shlomo, the town miser, caught wind of the tale, and hastened to the rabbi's home.

The rabbi peered suspiciously out from his door. "And what may I do for you?" he asked.

"I," the miser announced, in his most magnanimous voice, "am the friend of the friend of the friend who brought you the chicken last week." He pulled back his cloak, revealing a bowl and spoon, and pressed it into the rabbi's hand.

"By all means, come in," the rabbi gestured, "and sit down at my table while I prepare you a meal." The miser heard all sorts of noises in the kitchen—bowls rustling, knives chopping, stoves sputtering with fuel—and he savored the thought of his forthcoming feast.

At last the rabbi returned with Shlomo's bowl. The beggar eagerly took a sip, grimaced, and spat the liquid out. "What is this tasteless brew that you have served?" he disdainfully exclaimed.

The rabbi's eyes twinkled. "That, my dear Shlomo, is the broth of the broth of broth of my chicken soup!"

Selfishness, shall we say, brings with it a just dessert.

The story, of course, can be taken in many ways, and a variety morals could be made. Perhaps the tale speaks more deeply about the true nature of compassion, for isn't the clever rabbi teaching the miser an important lesson about himself? Others may find different lessons, for this is the beauty of a joke: the ending is always a surprise, and thus the diligent student can reexamine the habitual patterns of his thoughts.

Judaism, in particular, makes use of humorous tales, embedding layer upon layer of meaning into the script, to be pondered in one's personal search for truth. To struggle with God, one might say.

But the story of the rabbi and the chicken was devised for no such moral or point. I made it up specifically in response to another story I had written years ago, called "Gospel Soup," which I submitted to Miriyam Glazer for publication in this book. "But," she responded, "it's a *Christian* tale, and although it's funny and spiritually true, what does it have do with *Jewish* spirituality?

"It was written by Jew?" I meekly replied, but alas, she turned it down.

Until now.

One particular day God spoke to the Pope. It was an exhilarating experience and the Pope immediately went to tell the Bishop. "I have great news," he triumphantly announced, "for I have heard the Word of God!"

The Bishop went to the Deacon and proclaimed, "I have been given the Word of God, and I shall tell you what He has said." When he finished his story, the Deacon rushed to the Priest and announced, "I have received the Word of God, and now I shall give it to you."

The Priest gathered his congregation together and proclaimed the Word of God. A man stood up from his pew and loudly pronounced that the words had no substance. The congregation was shocked and demanded that the heretic be severely reprimanded.

Soon the entire community was in an uproar. The Deacon conferred with the Bishop and they decided to make a public example of him. They brought him in front of the entire assembly of the church elders. Even the Pope was present to hear the debate.

"You have been brought before us because you have claimed that the Word of God has no substance," the Bishop declared.

"No," said the man, "I have claimed that the words spoken by the priest have no substance."

"It is the same," countered the Deacon.

"No, it is not. It is the word of the word of the Word of God that I have heard."

"The content is still the same," argued the Priest, and the congregation cheered.

"If that is so, then I want you to drink the soup that I've prepared."

The crowd stirred at this eccentric request, but the Bishop was confident that the madness of this man would soon be exposed. "I will taste your gospel soup," he agreed.

He drank, then immediately frowned. "This soup has no flavor at all!"

"That is precisely my point," said the heretic. "I made this soup from the vegetables in my garden. Then I used this soup to make another soup, and from that soup I made another. Finally I used that soup to make a cauldron of liquid, large enough to serve every member in the congregation. It is the soup of the soup of the soup, yet you complain that it is tasteless because it has been so watered down. That, my dear Bishop, is what you have done with the Word of God!

The Pope himself blessed the man, and the story became a legend.

Different fable, different moral. Even pokes a little fun at the orthodoxy of the Church. But when I tried to turn it into a Jewish joke, I realized it wouldn't work—there just isn't a parallel priestly hierarchy in Judaism. I nearly gave up, until . . .

Enter the Mulla Nasrudin, a fictional dervish that appears in mystical Islamic tales. I came across my old copy of a book by Idries Shaw, which contained the unconscious roots of my gospel tale: a kinsman brings a duck to the Mulla Nasrudin, who shares it with his guest. Visitor after visitor then shows up at the Mulla's door, each expecting to be fed. Exasperated, the Mulla serves his latest his guest a bowl of hot water, proclaiming that it was "the soup of the soup of the soup of the duck that was brought by my relative."

Now I had the key to turning my gospel soup into a certifiably kosher meal. I could add meaning and context and metaphor, and garnish it with farfels à la Freud.

Spiritual wisdom has no borders or religious boundaries, and humor shall always be used to sneak in some deeper truth. For myself, all it took was a pinch of Christianity and a dash of Sufi wit to create a Jewish joke.

Mark Robert Waldman is the author of Love Games, Dreamscaping, *and* The Art of Staying Together. *He is a Woodland Hills therapist who lives in Malibu Lake, California.*

TOBIN BELZER

Ms. Identity Crisis

I sat in a circle, on a cool tile floor in Jerusalem, with twenty-one Jewish women from around the world. We would sit in that circle at least a hundred more times during the month that I participated in the Jewish Women's Leadership Project in Israel. After the first few days, our names and countries began to sound like a Miss Universe roll call: I am Lebana, from India; I am Ariella from Roma; I am Galia from Mexico City; I am Hedi from Finland. But each time I said I am Tobin from Los Angeles, I felt even more uncertain of who I really was. A Jew from a secular Jewish family . . . a Valley Girl who was living among East Coast intellectuals . . . a feminist who embraces her patriarchal religion. My contradictions felt irreconcilable.

I had incorrectly assumed that the Jewish Women's Leadership Project would be my opportunity to explore Israel from a feminist perspective. On the first day of the trip, though, when I noticed a few of the women trying not to stare at my unshaven legs, I had already felt it was time to worry. It was not going to be the trip I'd expected.

Yet for years I'd seen dozens of my friends return transformed from their youth group pilgrimage to Israel or their semester at Hebrew University. I'd watched their eyes gloss over with awe as they described their spiritually illuminating hikes through the Negev desert and their Shabbat dinners in Jerusalem. I'd seen hundreds of photographs of teens covered in Dead Sea mud or posed smiling in front of the Western Wall. True, I'd always been suspicious of their newfound religious convictions and had felt relieved when after a few weeks back in the States, they'd snapped out of it and stopped trying to keep kosher.

My friends had gone to Israel to mark the culmination of their years of

Jewish education. But by the time I got to Israel, I was no longer an undiscriminating teen. I had attended college at the University of Judaism in Los Angeles, with the goal of becoming a Jewish communal leader. But as we studied ancient, medieval, and modern Jewish civilization, the absence of women's voices in the curriculum had turned me onto feminism instead. After college, I went to graduate school in sociology and women's studies at Brandeis University and it was there I claimed my identity as a feminist sociologist.

Participating in the Jewish Women's Leadership Project in Israel, I had hoped to bridge my Judaism with my feminism among a group of women trying to do the same. That is, until I discovered that Evgenia from Latvia had never heard the word "feminist" before, and that our gender-segregated tour was the only one that Lebana from India's Orthodox father would allow her to attend. Our shared Jewishness and gender seemed insignificant compared to our cultural, political, and educational differences.

I felt completely alone.

I was angry at feminism for making me understand the biases against women in Judaism. I was furious at Judaism for having those biases. And I felt naive for having been so eager to learn Hebrew, so eager to be accepted as a Jew.

In the days that followed, I filled my travel diary with claims of betrayal, and chain-smoked Israeli cigarettes, enjoying the drama of self-torture. Needless to say, I was not easy to be around.

By the second week, I zealously rejected everything: Judaism, history, travel tours, Israel, and God. I started to refer to myself as an anti-Zionist heathen and with purposeful irreverence wrote God in my journal with a lowercase "g." I became convinced that the whole concept of God and the tale of the garden of Eden began with the fantasies of some very dehydrated and hallucinating men, who had wandered in the desert too long. Mischievously, I taught the Latvian women to say, "This sucks!" and encouraged them to say it often.

Our women-centered, gender-neutral, politically correct, and eco-sensitive Shabbat service made me furious. I saw no point in revising the prayers when all of Judaism was just part of an ancient patriarchal conspiracy and I'd prayed to that man-made God long enough. Besides, the majority of Jews (including some of the women in our group) would consider our feminist service heresy anyway.

I was as hard and as angry as the desert sun. I resolved that at the end of the trip, I would go back to Boston and find a group of Jews with whom I could reject Judaism.

By the third week I was exhausted. Reluctantly, I traveled with my group of Jewish Women Leaders to the Israel Museum. I sat on a bench in the "Jewish Heritage" section alone, watching a little girl skip carefree among the Torah scrolls encased in glass. Soon she too would discover how lowly women were in Judaism. I wept quietly for both of us.

I returned to the bus clutching my spiral notebook, with my face streaked with tears, too worn-out to isolate myself from the others. Julie and Elisheva sat down beside me and urged me to tell them what I had been writing about so passionately. Almost instantly a small group of women circled around me. They listening intently as I gave an impromptu reading from my journal:

My home is not in Judaism, I had written, *where as a woman I am excluded, insulted, and ignored by the traditions. I am not at home in the Jewish community, where I am judged by standards of observance that I do not meet. My home is not in Israel, where I feel so American and so white. My home is not in feminism, where I am perceived as a privileged, heterosexual Jew. My home is not in the San Fernando Valley, where my critique of class and gender inequality alienates me from my friends and family . . .*

To my amazement, they were nodding as I read. No sooner had I finished when one after another, they poured out their own stories: the tensions they felt between feminism and Judaism . . . the isolation, the split identities . . . whether in North America, South Africa, India, Australia. The more we talked, the more we discovered how alike we were and how much common ground we shared after all. I taught the Indian women to say, "Right on, sister!"

That Shabbat, in our youth hostel, we feasted on foods from the shuk, singing, talking, laughing, and eating, feeling the blessing of our new friendship. We had all felt alienated from our home communities. Here in Israel we were alienated from traditional Judaism. Yet in Israel, too, we had come together from four corners of the world and created a community with each other. Paradoxically, it was our own cultural, political, and educational differences that had helped us to realize the miracle of being able to identify ourselves in each other.

In the final days of the Jewish Women's Leadership Project, we held an impromptu talent swap to mark the end of our journey. The Indian women wore saris, and performed a traditional dance. The Mexican women sang a classical ranchera tune. Miriam gave us trinkets, which she'd brought with her from Australia. We danced to American pop music and ate humus and pita one last time together. The women who organized the trip gave out certificates to acknowledge each participant for her special contribution to the group. I was named, appropriately, "Ms. Identity Crisis."

Under the Jerusalem sky the night before we left, we gave blessings to one another. At that moment, I did feel blessed to have discovered this community of young Jewish women from across the globe who, like me, were searching for a community in which we can search for ourselves.

....

Tobin Belzer is a doctoral candidate in Women's Studies and Sociology at Brandeis University, and a Research Associate at the Hadassah Research Institute on Jewish Women. She is coeditor of On the Fringes: An Anthology of Young Jewish Women's Voices, *forthcoming from SUNY Press.*

KAREN ALKALAY-GUT

THE KEEPERS OF
MY YOUTH

I have now lost my barriers between me and death.
         —Jonathan Swift, on the loss of his mother

At the Jewish Old Age Home in my hometown,
the keepers of my youth sit in wheelchairs
sunning themselves in the crisp autumn air.

Shriveled hands grasp at my clothes as I pass:
my third-grade teacher, the doctor who set my arm
(broken from my first encounter with a bicycle),
the smiling crossing guard, my Hebrew school nurse.
Those who can speak and whose minds are clear
reminisce with tears in their eyes; others
look on and nod. "You played Haman in the Purim Spiel,"
rasps the accompanist from the Folk Shule,
"and now you are a grown-up lady
with teenage children of your own."
"Look how tall she is—from all the lunches
she ate at my house," my old friend's mother adds.

Here I am still in my flower. With a gentle hand
I smooth the shawls around their shoulders,
tuck the bright wool blankets into their chairs,
and whisper encouraging farewells to my troops at the front.

....

Karen Alkalay-Gut's recent books of poetry include Ignorant Armies *(Cross-Cultural Communications, 1994), and* Recipes: Love Soup and Other Poems *(Yaron Golan). She has translated many Israeli poets, and been awarded the BBC World Service Poetry Award, the Golan Poetry Award, and The Rachel Prize. She lives in Tel Aviv.*

FOOD FOR THOUGHT

There's a famous cooking story which goes like this:

A young woman asks her mother how to make a brisket. "First," says the mother, "you buy a whole brisket from the butcher and bring it home. Then, you immediately cut off the bottom end, which looks like a triangle, and throw it away. You put the remaining brisket in a roasting pan with spices, salt and pepper, on very high heat and braise the outside for about 15 minutes to sear the fat. Lower the heat and cook slowly for many hours with a little liquid (wine or catsup do nicely) and sliced onions, until the meat almost falls apart. That's how you make a brisket."

The young woman did as her mother said, and for many years brought home the huge slab of beef, cut off the lower triangle and threw it away, before putting it into the roaster, and so on. The results were delicious, but the woman was puzzled. One day, her grandmother came to visit and saw the woman preparing brisket. Once again, she cut off the lower tip and threw it away.

"Why are you throwing away perfectly good meat?" the grandmother asked.

"That's what my mother told me to do. It's part of the ritual which makes the brisket so tasty."

"Ridiculous," said the older woman. "She saw me do the same thing for years. But I had a reason. I never had a pan big enough to hold a whole brisket, so I had to cut off the end so the meat would fit."

Here's a story of my own.

When I was a child, my mother made blintzes from scratch, making a big batch for the freezer, enough to last a year.

Out came the huge black cast-iron pan, the flour and eggs for the crepe batter, and the farmer cheese for the filling. Then she took out two old linen dish towels and laid them on the kitchen counter. I could hear it from my bedroom: the sizzle of the batter gliding into the pan, then a huge bang of the pan against the tabletop as the crepe was flipped onto the towel. And finally a little sigh of satisfaction as the crepes piled up. Sizzle, bang, sigh. Sizzle, bang, sigh. In my memory, making blintzes was as arduous and treacherous as digging a ditch.

Even when I had my own family, I dared not try to make blintzes. I didn't have the right dish towels. And I wasn't "old" enough or strong enough to lift the heavy pan.

"Nonsense," said my husband, a crepe master of wide repute. And he started to show me. If the pan was well greased with melted butter, there was no bang at all, only the smooth gliding sound of a crepe falling onto wax paper.

"Stop!" I cried out. "This isn't right!" I went to the linen closet and took out two old clean pillow cases. I took the pan and started banging. "I don't have the linen towels, so these will have to do!"

The big questions of adult life are not so much about right and wrong. They are, more often, about cold versus warmth, meaning versus emptiness, freedom versus oppression, connection versus isolation. That's why I cook: to feel warm, have meaning, feel free, and make connections, more often around holiday time, but whenever the feeling strikes. When I cook I feel certain something is going to happen. This is important because often in adult life nothing much happens, not for a long time at any rate, and sometimes what happens won't be good.

But with food there's always a chance. I will cook. You will eat. You will smile. I will be happy. Life can be a dream.

Some years ago, seemingly out of the blue, I started making gefilte fish. No one I knew had ever made it before, so it wasn't like I was following my grandmother's tradition or anything like that. And I had plenty else to do, believe me. Still, the inspiration could not be silenced. I needed a different kind of connection to Passover, a connection beyond intellect, one that had less to do with my own specific past than to a world-weary *shtetl* gone for good. Fish, I thought. Jewish women once made their own fish. I will make my own fish, too.

It's amazing how these impulses take over, the compulsion to eat and cook ritual foods which have no intrinsic spiritual meaning. Beyond challah and matzah, no specific foods are commanded of Jews to eat. Many foods are forbidden, but where is it written that every Jewish function has chocolate chip rugelach and pound cake?

Thefact is that food is ritual, or at least a lead-in to ritual, and without ritual we would continue to eat, but without eating, most rituals would die. That's why I respect those so-called deli-catessen Jews whose only link is corned beef on rye or a good onion roll. Through their deli order they ask: Where do I fit in? What must I cut off? What can I carry along from the past? And do I have the right to throw out what is stale and seek something fresh? And these are the questions which count. Given half a chance, we can all be what we eat, and a good onion roll, even today, is hard to find.

GEFILTE FISH
(written with the accent as your grandmother would tell it to you.)

So I make fish, and this is what I learned. It is hard work. And not cheap. You start off thinking that is should only take two hours, but it takes all day. Nevertheless it's a task I love doing.

I use a mix of whitefish, pike, and carp (ask for six pounds finished, and extra heads and tails for the stock).

The Stock: First you make a soup out of fish heads and tails, 2 stalks celery, sliced, 2 carrots sliced, and 5 sliced onions, 1 tablespoon salt. Cover with three quarts of water and bring to a boil.

The Fish: Next, you make fluffy fish balls (like matzah balls for soup). No, I don't grind it myself, nor is there a carp in my bathtub. The fish man grinds it for me. Do I feel guilty? Only as guilty as I feel that the meat man grinds my hamburger rather than making me kill the cow myself.

Mix the ground fish with 1 large finely ground onion, 4 eggs, and 6 slices challah or 3 tablespoons matzah meal with ½ cup water, 1 tablespoon salt, and 1 teaspoon ground white pepper and ¼ cup oil. Begin to form the egg-shaped balls (about a cup of fish mixture) and drop them into the stock. Moisten hands in ice water so they don't stick. Soon you will sweat, and your hands will shrivel from soaking in ice water, but at least the fish balls don't stick to you. Drop the fish balls into the hot stock. Add more sliced carrots on top. Cover and cook 1½ hours.

Remove cover for the last half hour. Strain stock over fish. Chill. Serve on lettuce topped with fish broth and carrots.

Just as you're wondering why you're going through this sweaty ordeal, the magic begins. You feel the imaginary babushka on your head tying back your imaginary long dark hair. The walls of your American adobe home are replaced by the brick walls of the European ghetto and up on the roof you hear Isaac Stern and his violin. That night, everyone at your table will marvel how you, a modern career woman, have miraculously turned into a gefilte-fish maker of the 19th century. If you've made fresh horseradish, your guests may be moved to tears.

Your friends will smile.
You will smile.
Life will be a dream.

April 1994

Marlene Marks

....

Marlene Marks is the author of A Woman's Voice *(On the Way Press, 1998) and the editor of* Nice Jewish Girls Growing Up in America *(Penguin, 1996). A journalist and syndicated columnist, she lives in Malibu, California.*

THE GARDEN

Adam and Eve were exiled from the Garden of Eden. And they lived together east of Eden, tilling the earth, raising children, struggling to stay alive. After the years of struggle, when their children were grown, they decided to see the world.

They journeyed from one corner of the world to the other. Wandering from place to place, in the course of their journeys, they discovered the entrance to the Garden of Eden, now guarded by an angel with a flaming sword. Frightened, they began to flee when suddenly God spoke to them:

"Adam and Eve, you have lived in exile these many many years. The punishment is complete. You may return now to the Garden."

As the words were spoken, the angel with his flaming sword disappeared and the gate to the Garden opened. "Come in, Adam. Come in, Eve."

"Wait," Adam replied. "You know, it has been so many years. Remind me, what is it like in the Garden?"

"The Garden is paradise!" God responded. "In the Garden there is no work. Neither of you need ever struggle or toil again. There is no pain, no suffering. No death. Life goes on forever, day after day. Come, return to the Garden!"

Adam and Eve listened to God's words—no work, no struggle, no pain, no death. An endless life of perpetual ease. And then Adam turned and looked at Eve. He looked at the woman with whom he had struggled to make a life, to take bread from the earth, to raise children, to build a home. He thought of the tragedies they had overcome and the joys they cherished.

And Adam shook his head, "no, thank you, that's not for me . . . Come on Eve, let's go."

Adam and Eve turned their backs on Paradise, and hand in hand, they walked home.

Ed Feinstein serves as a rabbi of Valley Beth Shalom in Encino, California, and as a lecturer in the Ziegler School of Rabbinic Studies at the University of Judaism in Los Angeles. His Torah commentaries appear in the Los Angeles Jewish Journal. *Well known for his storytelling, Rabbi Feinstein is reputed to bake the best challach west of the Rio Grande, according to wife Rabbi Nina Feinstein and children Yonah (14), Nessa (11), and Raphael (8).*

⊙ur Angels

Our angels
Spend much of their time sleeping
In their dreams
They tear down the new houses by the sea
And build old ones
In their place.

No matter how long they may sleep
One hundred two hundred years
Ten centuries is not too much
The first to wake up
Takes the torch that has been handed down
Adds a drop of oil to the lamp
Blesses the eternal light
And then recalls the name
Of every other angel
And one by one as they are remembered
They wake up

For them
As for us
There is nothing more beautiful
Than memory.

Howard Schwart

Howard Schwartz's poem was first published in Vessels *(Unicorn Press, 1977). His other books of poetry are* Gathering the Sparks *(Singing Wind, 1979) and* Sleepwalking Beneath the Stars *(BkMk Press, 1992).*

Glossary One

THE CAST OF CHARACTERS

Rabbi Akiva: (c. 50–135 C.E.) Akiva ben Joseph began as a poor, illiterate shepherd, and with the encouragement and support of his wife, Rachel, eventually became one of the greatest scholars and most influential figures in early Judaism. He was tortured to death by the Romans, who had issued an edict forbidding the study of Torah.

The Ba'al Shem Tov: (1700–1760) Israel ben Eliezer, known as the *Ba'al Shem Tov* or its acronym, the *"Besht"* ("Master of the Good Name"), was the founder of Hasidism, the mystical movement in which fervent and joyous prayer took precedence over religious scholarship. Hundreds of Hasidic tales tell about his adventures, teachings, wisdom.

Rabbi Moses ben Jacob Cordovero: (1522–1570) Of Spanish origin, Moses Cordovero was an exemplary Kabbalist in Safed (Tsfat). His most influential works include *Pardes Rimmonim* (Cracow, 1592), *Elimah Rabbati* (Lvov, 1881), as well as commentaries on the Zohar, the central mystical text of Kabbalah. He summarized and charted the development of trends in the Kabbalah, and attempted to construct a system for Kabbalistic thought.

Rabbi Eliezer ben Azariah: (1st–2nd c. C.E.) A priest, Eliezer was a descendent of the prophet Ezra, and served as the head of the Sanhedrin. It was Eliezar who defined a quality of Yom Kippur that continues to be central to Jewish observance today: "The Day of Atonement can bring forgiveness for transgressions between man and the Almighty, but not for transgressions between one man and another until the one has obtained the other's pardon" *(Yoma 8:9).*

Rabbi Israel ben Ze'ev Wolf Lipkin (Salanter): (1810–1883) A disciple of Rabbi Zundel of Salant, Israel Lipkin founded and became the spiritual father of Musar, the movement within Judaism dedicated to rigorous ethical and moral standards. He was a pioneer in both scholarly and civic spheres, proposing that the Talmud be translated into Hebrew and European languages; that it be printed in one volume; and that it be taught in universities.

Rabbi Shimon ben Zoma: (2nd c. C.E.) A contemporary of Akiva, Ben Zoma is referred to as an authority on Mishnah, though in his time he was regarded only as a disciple. An exemplary scholar, many of his sayings became proverbs, and it was said that his appearances in dreams brought wisdom to the dreamer.

Resh Lakish: (3rd c. C.E.) Resh Lakish is an acronym of Rabbi Simeon ben Lakish. A friend and brother-in-law of Yochanan, Resh Lakish was known for his honesty and integrity in mundane matters. Perhaps that's ironic, because Resh Lakish was seen by his contemporaries also as a troublemaker; to earn a living, he temporarily abandoned his studies to become a gladiator, and was rumored to associate with thieves. He claimed that the Book of Job was a work of fiction, intended only as a moral lesson.

Rabbi Yochanan: (3rd c. C.E.) An editor of the Jerusalem Talmud. Brother-in-Law of Resh Lakish, and a pupil of Simeon bar Eleazar, Yochanan declared that the rabbinic commandments of the Mishnah were as crucial as the laws given to Moses on Mount Sinai. Fascinating descriptions of his handsomeness abound; according to the Talmud *(Bava Metzia 84a)*, he himself said: "I am the only one remaining of Jerusalem's men of outstanding beauty. He who desires to see Rabbi Yochanan's beauty, let him take a silver goblet as it emerges from the crucible, fill it with the seeds of red pomegranate, encircle its brim with a chaplet of red roses, and set in between the sun and the shade: its lustrous glow is akin to Rabbi Yochanan's beauty."

Zusia: (Meshulam Zusia, of Hanipoli; d. 1800) An early leader of
Hasidism and a renowned disciple of "the Maggid of Mezerich,"
Dov Baer, Zusia plays the role of a benevolent, simple, and
righteous hero in many Hasidic folktales. Though often depicted as
unsophisticated, Zusia's own writings on Torah are serious works of
scholarship.

Glossary Two

WORDS AND PHRASES

Aliyah: (Hebrew) literally, to "go up." To make *aliyah* is to immigrate to Israel.

Amidah: a silent prayer of supplication, recited while standing, central to Jewish liturgy.

Beit midrash: (Hebrew) a religious study hall.

Bobe: (Yiddish) grandmother.

Bobe-mayse: (Yiddish) an old wives' tale.

Brit/Bris: (Hebrew/Yiddish) circumcision.

Challah: (Hebrew) traditional braided bread, served on the Sabbath and festivals.

Chametz: (Hebrew) food which has been leavened, and is hence forbidden on Passover.

Cheder: (Hebrew & Yiddish) in Hebrew, literally "a room." Pronounced *chay'der* it means a school for children's religious study.

Chesed: (Hebrew) loving-kindness.

Chutzpah: (Hebrew & Yiddish) nerve.

Daven/doven: (Hebrew/Yiddish) to pray.

Dreidel: a spinning top with four sides, used to play a game on Hanukkah.

Dybbuk: a demon that takes possession of another's body.

Galabiyah: a loose-fitting dresslike garment traditionally worn by men in the Middle East.

Haggadah: in Hebrew, literally, "The Telling"; the guide to the Passover seder, with songs, commentary, stories.

Halutznikot: (Hebrew) women pioneers.

Hanukkah: a holiday which lasts eight days, and celebrates the triumph of the Maccabees, in rescuing and resanctifying the Temple in Jerusalem from the Greeks in 164 B.C.E.

Hasid: (Hebrew) literally, "a pious man." A follower of Hasidim, the fervent religious movement originating in the 18th century.

Has v'halilah: (Hebrew) the equivalent of "God forbid!"

Hatikvah: in Hebrew, literally, "the Hope"; Israel's National Anthem.

Kabbalah: the mystical tradition of Jerusalem, as evolved in many texts, commentaries, systems of thought, over hundreds of generations.

Kashrut: (Hebrew) kosher; in accordance with Jewish dietary law.

Kinder: (Yiddish) a child.

Kohelet: (Hebrew) Ecclesiastes.

Lag B'Omer: for seven weeks from the second night of Passover until Shavuot (a time of harvest, the Time of the Giving of the Torah, Pentecost), a ritual known as the "Counting of the Omer" takes place. Literally, *Omer* means "measure," and refers to the offering of the first of the new grain harvest that was taken to the Temple. But the period of the Omer also corresponds spiritually to the time between the liberation from slavery (Passover) and the Receiving of the Torah (Shavuot). Since the destruction of the Temple, the "Counting of the Omer" has thus evolved into a spiritually significant process, particularly in the mystical tradition. Lag B'Omer is the thirty-third day of the Omer (LG=33 in Hebrew); mourning rituals associated with the Omer period for various reasons are suspended and, in Israel, festivities take place in honor of Rabbi Shimon bar Yochai at Meron.

Maggid: a traditional Jewish storyteller.

Mamale: (Yiddish) literally, "little mother"; mommy.

Marranos: Spanish and Portuguese Jews who, in order to escape persecution and execution during the Inquisition, outwardly converted to Christianity, while maintaining their Judaism in secret.

Matzah: unleavened bread eaten on Passover.

Mazel: (Yiddish; Hebrew: mazal) luck.

Mea She'arim: the ultra-Orthodox Jewish neighborhood of Jerusalem.

Menorah: a candelabra, typically used on Hanukkah.

Menschlekeit: (Yiddish) good-heartedness.

Midrash: from the Hebrew *drsh*, "to examine carefully," *Midrash* is the vast body of biblical commentary, guided by strict rules of interpretation (hermeneutics), written by the rabbis of the Mishnah, Talmud, and later generations. Applied to strictly legal portions of the Bible, they became *midrash halakhah;* to narrative material, *midrash aggadah.* The latter seeks particularly to explain, expand, develop, and uncover the hidden spiritual meaning in the laconic Biblical text. In recent years, the term has assumed a less formal meaning; *midrash* has increasingly been used as the near equivalent of "storytelling," when the story spun has its origins in a biblical text.

Mikveh: a ritual purification bath.

Mincha: evening prayer.

Minyan: the ten people required to hold a prayer service.

Mishnah: the collection of decrees, or *halachot*, which evolved from oral law, on which the Talmud is based.

Mourner's Kaddish: a daily prayer which includes praise and thanksgiving, and is recited by mourners on behalf of the departed.

Parsha: the "portion" into which the Torah is divided (as distinct from "chapter.

Passover: the springtime holiday which celebrates and symbolically reenacts the liberation of the Hebrews from slavery in Pharaoh's *Mizrayim.*

Phylacteries: "And it shall be for a sign unto you upon your hand, and for a memorial between your eyes, that the Lord's law may be in your mouth: for with a strong hand the Lord brought you out of Egypt" (Exod. 13:9). Exodus 13:1–10 and 11–16, as well as Deut. 6:4–9 and 11:13–21, are inscribed on parchment in the *tefillin*, the phylacteries, consisting of *shel rosh*, the small leather vessel bound onto the head, and the *shel yod*, that bound onto the hand, to fulfill the commandment. The phylacteries/*tefillin* are worn during prayer every morning except Sabbath and festivals.

Rebbe: (Yiddish) a rabbi.

Seder: the ritual Passover meal.

Shabbat: (Hebrew) the Jewish Sabbath, which begins on Friday at sundown, and concludes when three stars appear in the sky on Saturday night.

Shacharit: morning paper.

Shammas: the Hanukkah candle used to light each of the other eight candles.

Shiva: the weeklong mourning ritual.

Shmata: (Yiddish) an old rag.

Shmutz: (Yiddish) dirt.

Shtetl: (Yiddish) a rural village (where millions of eastern European Jews lived prior to World War II).

Shuk: (Hebrew) an open-air marketplace.

Shul: (Yiddish) the synagogue.

Tallit/tallis: (Yiddish and Hebrew) the fringed prayer shawl.

Talmud: the accumulated books of Jewish ceremonial and civil oral law, and its interpretation by the ancient Sages. The Talmud is comprised of the Mishnah and the Gemara, or commentary on the Mishnah. It evolved in both Babylonia (200–500 C.E.) and in Palestine (200–350 C.E.), and hence there are two versions—the Babylonian and the Palestinian, or Jerusalem, Talmud.

Torah: the "Five Books of Moses"—the first five books of the Hebrew Bible, from *B'reshit*/Genesis, to *Sh'mot*/Exodus, *Vayikra*/Leviticus, *B'midbar*/Numbers, and *D'varim*/Deuteronomy. "Torah," however, which comes from the same root as "Teaching," is also used to mean the *whole way of Judaism*, the whole body of Jewish knowledge and wisdom.

Treif: (Yiddish) nonkosher food.

T'shuvah: (Hebrew) literally, "return" or "answer." Figuratively, repentance.

Tzaddik: (Hebrew) a holy man.

Western Wall: the last remaining wall from the ancient Temple site in Jerusalem. The second Temple was destroyed in 70 C.E.

Yad VaShem: in Hebrew, literally "the Hand and the Name"; the memorial to the Shoah in Jerusalem.

Yahrzeit: the anniversary of a death.

Yeshiva: a school for intensive religious study.

Yidele: (Yiddish) literally, "little Jew."

Zohar: literally, "The Book of Splendor"; the central mystical text of Kabbalah traditionally attributed to Rabbi Shimon bar Yochai. From a scholarly perspective, the Zohar is a vast and complex literary anthology which consists of sections from several different sources.

About the Editor

Miriyam Glazer has loved stories since she was a little girl and her mother read to her every night from the *Home University Bookshelf*. Her father regaled her with stories of his youthful motorcycle adventures, and her Hebrew School principal mesmerized her with the power of the stories in the Torah. Not surprisingly, Glazer became a professor of literature at Ben Gurion University in Beersheva, Israel, where she lived for eleven years. Since 1988, she has been teaching at the University of Judaism in Los Angeles, where she is also the director of the Dortort Writers Institute.

A popular speaker throughout the United States, she has published many essays on new Jewish fiction, written personal memoirs, and translated Hebrew poetry. Her anthology, *Burning Air and a Clear Mind*, introduced Israeli women poets to the English-speaking audience for the first time. Glazer's newest collection, *Dreaming the Actual: Contemporary Fiction and Poetry by Israeli Women Writers*, will be released this spring.

Permissions

Miriyam Glazer, "War and Peace" and "Dancing on the Edge of the World" © 1999 by Miriyam Glazer.

Karen Golden, "The Legacy" © 1999 by Karen Golden.

Sarah Graff, "Spiritual Secrets" © by Sarah Graff.

Daniel Greyber, ".08 of a Second" © 1999 by Daniel Greyber.

Jill Hammer, "Yehi Meorot Barakia: 'Let There Be Lights in the Expanse'" © 1999 by Jill Hammer.

Rodger Kamenetz, "Rye" and "The Broken Tablets" © 1999 by Rodger Kamenetz.

Irena Klepfisz, "*Di yerushe* / The Legacy: A Parable About History and *Bobe-mayses, Barszcz,* and *Borsht* and the Future of the Jewish Past." © Irena Klepfisz. Originally published in *Prairie Schooner.*

Label Lam, "The Wallet and the Cold Toe" © 1999 by Project Genesis, @ Torah.org.

Michael Lerner, "God's House" © 1999 by Michael Lerner.

Richard N. Levy, "Shabbat: An Encounter in the Apple Grove" © 1999 by Richard N. Levy.

Marlene Marks, "How a Single Mom does Shabbat" and "Food for Thought," © 1998 by Marlene Adler Marks. Originally published in *A Woman's Voice* (On the Way Press).

Ilyse Mimoun, "The Jewish Bite" © 1999 by Ilyse Mimoun.

Jonathan Omer-Man, "Fish: A Story" © Jonathan Omer-Man.

Freema Gottleib, "In Days Gone By and in Our Own Time." From *The Lamp of God* by Freema Gottleib. Reprinted by permission of the publisher, Jason Aronson, Inc., Northvale, NJ © 1989.

Paysach J. Krohn, Adaptations of "United in Parcel Service," "Perfection at the Plate," and "Plane and Simple" from *Echoes of the Maggid* by Rabbi Paysach J. Krohn. Reprinted by permission of Artscroll/Mesorah Publications, Ltd. © 1999.